MAN

—versus—

BALL

Related Titles from Potomac Books

Tailgate to Heaven: A British NFL Fan Tackles America
    by Adam Goldstein

Baseball's Most Wanted™: The Top 10 Book of the National Pastime's
    Outrageous Offenders, Lucky Bounces, and Other Oddities
    by Floyd Conner

Football's Most Wanted™: The Top 10 Book of the Great Game's Outrageous
    Characters, Fortunate Fumbles, and Other Oddities
    by Floyd Conner

King of Clubs: The Great Golf Marathon of 1938
    by Jim Ducibella

The Year That Changed the Game: The Memorable Months
    That Shaped Pro Football
    by Jonathan Rand

MAN
—versus—
BALL

ONE ORDINARY GUY AND HIS
EXTRAORDINARY
SPORTS ADVENTURES

JON HART

Potomac Books
Washington, D.C.

Library of Congress Cataloging-in-Publication Data
Hart, Jon, 1968–
Man versus ball : one ordinary guy and his extraordinary sports adventures / Jon Hart.
  pages cm
ISBN 978-1-61234-414-0 (hardcover : alk. paper)
ISBN 978-1-61234-415-7 (electronic)
  1. Athletes—Psychology. 2. Sports—Psychological aspects. I. Title.
GV706.4.H39 2013
796.01'9—dc23

                                                2013000754

Printed in the United States of America on acid-free paper that meets the American National Standards Institute Z39-48 Standard.

Potomac Books
22841 Quicksilver Drive
Dulles, Virginia 20166

First Edition

10 9 8 7 6 5 4 3 2 1

For everyone who didn't get in the game

CONTENTS

ACKNOWLEDGMENTS

I'm very grateful to my editor, Elizabeth Demers, and everyone at Potomac Books for making this book come to fruition. I wish to express my gratitude to my agent, John Talbot, for his advocacy and guidance. I also wish to thank my friend Dorothy Gannon, a talented writer who carefully read over the manuscript and provided invaluable feedback. During the proposal stage, Jill Rothenberg gave wonderful input.

To reach the finish line, I also had support from the following: Jennifer Bruno, Alan Charles, Rob Farbman, Mark Hill, Kenny Hoberman, Tom Kearns, Larry Koffler, Johnny Lampert, Randall Lane, Louie Max, Hank Owenmark, Greg Senf, and Brad Trackman.

Last, I want to thank my parents, who probably wished I didn't do any of this stuff. Regardless, none of it would have been possible without them.

PRE GAME

I never saw the hit coming. I don't recall lying facedown in the dirt. I don't remember getting strapped on to the stretcher and being rolled off the field. When I finally came to in the hospital's emergency room, I felt like David Byrne. "What have I done? How did I get here?" I might've mumbled to the nurse.

═══

Growing up in New York City, I didn't see too many white picket fences. I was surrounded by concrete. Sure, there were some fields, but they were often rock hard and littered with broken bottles. There was no Little League. After school, I played on the sidewalk outside my apartment building, dodging pedestrians and cars when the ball went into traffic. We had an eclectic crew. The Hispanic guy was called Fido. The Buddhist kid knew karate and wasn't shy about using it. The black dude always carried a tennis racket, but I never saw him on an actual court. A few times, the Hasidic kids from around the corner would challenge us to a game.

When my father returned home from work with the paper, it was cause for minor celebration. We both loved the sports pages. I wasn't a stats guy. I enjoyed the wonderful personalities, from Reggie to Billy to Clyde. Early on, I wasn't sure if I wanted to be a player or the guy that got to write about the great characters.

Every so often, my father would regale me with tales about a unique man named George Plimpton, who took on athletic challenges and wrote about them. Plimpton had participated in a Detroit Lions training camp, played with the Boston Bruins, and sparred with a professional boxer or

1

two, among other endeavors. Early on, I knew that my abilities wouldn't get me to the Majors. I could get hit by a baseball, but I couldn't hit a baseball with the bat. However, I possessed great balance and a natural knack for roller skating, and with all its concrete, NYC was a roller skating paradise. I had the potential to make it in the roller derby—or perform with the Ice Capades. Sadly, roller derby was no longer around, and I don't do leotards. But maybe, just maybe, I could follow Plimpton's path.

For the moment, I took the conventional route—playing soccer in high school. We won few games, but my enthusiasm was rewarded by the newly formed cheerleading squad, who asked me to be their first and only male cheerleader.

To this day, I regret not taking them up on their offer.

At the University of Vermont, I took up rugby, which is often referred to as "elegant violence." Rugby is as elegant as a barroom brawl. Since I had long displayed a penchant for running into immobile objects, it seemed like a perfect fit. In my first game, I broke my nose. More than the actual game, which is basically Kill the Carrier with a few rules, I loved the guys on the team, despite the fact that they didn't say much. Between grunts, they barked encouragement. "Suck it up!" was the most common command. I had never heard this expression before, but I started using it at every opportunity. You don't like the reading assignment? *Suck it up!* You don't like the cafeteria food? *Suck it up!* The rugby guys had great names: Eichler, Swifty, Chic, EB, and Spangler. Spangler was the baddest of the badasses. He had piercing eyes, never smiled, and if he spoke, I never heard it. There was a wrestling club at Vermont. Spangler was its sole member. Even the other rugby guys were intimidated by him.

After getting knocked out and retiring from rugby, I wanted to share my thoughts on the ruggers with a wider audience, so I headed over to the school newspaper, the *Vermont Cynic*, and volunteered to cover the relatively little-known sport. Fortunately, they needed writers and published my columns. In my first piece, I revealed that the team was petrified of Spangler. This didn't win me any awards, but my columns did get Spangler to crack a smile, and he did talk to me. I had found my niche.

After graduating Phi Beta Sugarbush, between different jobs to pay the bills, I continued on Plimpton's path, participating in athletic events and writing about the experiences. By this point, it was the natural thing to do. I arm-wrestled, ran a race in the middle of the night, and started playing basketball—on in-line skates. I was chasing adventures and bylines, not always in that order. It was a "chicken and egg" thing. The adventures inspired me to write, and the writing inspired me to be adventurous. I needed both. It was a package deal. Without one or the other, I was just a guy on the couch eating chips and talking fantasy league. Just one problem with that scenario: I don't play fantasy league!

With all that in mind, this isn't your typical sports book.

It's not about superstars or championship teams. There are plenty of great books about that stuff. I haven't played in the NFL or the Major Leagues. I've never made it to the Olympics—not even as a spectator. However, I've competed on the fields less played on and developed a bucket list of unique sports adventures.

Feel free to pass the chips!

1
Plimpton

When we're forced to kick off, there are just eleven seconds left in the half. Our kicker, a former college All-American, is supposed to kick the ball just over 10 yards on the ground to the left. It's a squib kick, designed to waste time, so that the half will end without incident. We line up and wait for All-American to approach the ball. "Full speed!" yells Rambo, a wild-eyed teammate who pounds his thigh pads with his fists for emphasis. As All-American runs toward the ball, my teammates and I follow, advancing down the field. And then everything goes awry.

Instead of booting the ball into the ground as directed, All-American whales into it. "What the fuck!" someone mutters. I watch the ball go end over end before disappearing into the pitch-black sky as I run as hard as I possibly can. Rambo won't have anything to complain about. I can't locate the ball, though, and then everything goes blank.

And it stays that way.

———

Initially, I had no plans to play semi-pro football. I just wanted to write a profile on the Brooklyn Mariners and their colorful coach, Pudgie Walsh. After learning about the Mariners from a childhood friend who played for Pudgie, I wrote about the team for a small publication. A few years later, Pudgie and his squad still intrigued me, and I pitched the idea to a well-known and widely read publication. I was optimistic that they'd assign me the story. I waited and waited, and finally they ran a lengthy front-page profile on Pudgie and the Mariners—with someone else's by-line. Unfortunately, they had intercepted my idea and assigned it to one of their regular contributors.

While discouraged, I still wanted to cover Pudgie and the Mariners. Unfortunately for me, the article had been seen by just about everyone. If I didn't want to be a copycat, I had to come up with a new wrinkle. It was just the excuse I needed. I'd join the team and become a Mariner—not for a play or a game, but for an entire season. Full speed.

=====

We meet in Marine Park, deep in southern Brooklyn, at the Mariner Inn, a low-key street corner bar that serves as Pudgie's office. It's off the beaten path, a haul from the bright lights of Midtown Manhattan. When I walk through the Inn's door, I pass a display of Mariners photos, which cover the bar's wood-paneled walls. In the empty backroom of the bar, I take a seat across from the Mariners' legendary coach, and we get down to it.

"I want to be a Mariner."

Pudgie, a sixty-six-year-old retired firefighter and a leprechaun of a man, eyes my solid but relatively unimposing 190-pound, *almost* 5-foot-10 frame. Lately, I've been doing more running and in-line skating than pumping iron. I'm more stubborn than strong.

"You want to get killed," shoots back Pudgie, whose voice one reporter described as a cross between a Vienna choir boy and Bruce Springsteen.

Eventually, we reach this agreement: if I agree to be the team's press relations representative, I can be on the team.

I aspired to be a flanker. I wound up being a flack.

Nevertheless, I'm on the team. The meeting is a touchdown.

=====

In late spring, I show up for pre-season practice at Kings Bay Field, the Mariners' home turf, adjacent to a massive fortress, which I'm told is a sewage facility. It's a decent field as far as fields go, but there's absolutely nothing professional about it. It doesn't matter. I'm here to play.

Years ago, I used to play. As a kid, I spent countless hours tackling all comers in my room and playing touch on the narrow streets of my neighborhood. For a few seasons, I even played on a tackle football team, until my parents put a kibosh on that. They preferred non-contact pursuits, such as oboe lessons and other hobbies that, well, didn't interest me. Now, with my youth vanishing by the minute, I'm finally going for gridiron glory. It's fourth down. Actually, it's beyond that. It's fifth down.

While I have had minimal experience, most of the hundred or so hopefuls had played some sort of organized ball. Over the years, the Mariners had played in professional leagues like the now-defunct USFL, the CFL (in Canada), and one of the professional indoor leagues. As far as the grandest stage, a few Mariners had made it to training camp and a small handful even played during the NFL's 1988 strike season. However, no Mariner has ever stepped on the field during an official NFL game. Now, on the eve of another new season, a few of the Mariners' pro football aspirations have been revitalized. Wrestling impresario Vince McMahon is starting a new league, the XFL. As for the others, probably the vast majority, they're not making a career move by playing for the Mariners. They just want to play some ball and knock heads, not necessarily in that order.

While some of the Mariners weigh their professional football options, I have other concerns: I need a position. There's no shortage of sleek wide receivers and defensive backs, and I don't think I'm quite ready for the pressure of being a running back, plus the Mariners are loaded at that position. So I opt to work out with a small group of four bulky linemen. In this intimate group, I figure that I'll get some much-needed personal attention. Besides a few games of two-hand touch, I haven't picked up an actual football in years. With these guys, I won't have to worry about touching the ball. These humble, meaty specimens never get the ball, never score, and never get the glory. "You're in the trenches," declares the line coach, a supersized, affable man who sucks on a cigar as if it's a slab of licorice. We practice coming off the line of scrimmage and pounding into a pad, which the coach holds. "First contact—make a statement, tell him, you're messing with a tough sonuvabitch!" the coach growls. Later, the coach offers me this advice: "Gain a hundred pounds before the opening game." The Mariners linemen aren't slouches in the size department, averaging 6-foot-3 and 300 pounds. Pudgie refers to these monstrosities as the Moose. Not only large, the Moose are very experienced. Like many of the Mariners, they're mostly in their late twenties and thirties, so they've been around, and playing ball is second nature.

Throughout the summer, we practice under Kings Bay's lights every Wednesday night. Practice is supposed to start at eight, but it usually gets going around eight thirty. Attendance is encouraged but not required. No one is getting a cent to play, and everyone has a job or is trying to get one. The Mariners work as cops, salesmen, computer engineers, firemen, finance guys, bartenders, and cable guys, among other things. One guy works as a stripper. Another is a caddie. I've got a steady gig as a copywriter. (I haven't conducted a poll, but I'm probably the only copywriter on the squad.) Practices are mostly low-key, casual affairs, with the team practicing formations and running plays. Contact is absolutely forbidden. No one can risk injury. If there's an injury, it's going to happen during an actual game. There's no Mariners team physician. In the teeth department, however, we're all set. The Mariners have a dentist, or rather someone training to be a dentist, on the roster. Also, before joining the Fire Department, Pudgie was a naval dental technician, and after serving he sold dental supplies.

Into the summer, we sprint and do calisthenics—no pads. I dance around cones and crash into tackling dummies with everything I got. Unfortunately, I'm quicker with ideas than my feet. While I work out, I hear a voice that sounds vaguely like a Vienna choir boy's. "Keep your head up, Plimpton," Pudgie mutters. I don't really have a position, but I do have a nickname. With increasing frequency, Pudgie refers to me as "Plimpton," as in George Plimpton, the journalist who wrote *Paper Lion*, the book that chronicles his experiences with the Detroit Lions. Plimpton's exploits had always resonated with me, and they offered a secondary plan: if my athletic ability wasn't quite there, I could always get on a team by writing about it. Until the Mariner Inn bartender compared me to Plimpton, Pudgie had never heard of him. Now, Pudgie's taken with the name, specifically with the way it sounds, and he can't keep himself from saying it.

Pudgie bellows Plimpton!
Pudgie growls Plimpton!
Pudgie screams Plimpton!

Pudgie whispers Plimpton!
Pudgie yells Plimpton!
If Pudgie could, he'd yodel Plimpton!

I'm not a football player. I'm fodder for Pudgie's opera.

Many, if not almost all, of the Mariners believe that Plimpton is my actual name. Some are just confused. One guy questions me about the name's origin. "Is he a singer?" he asks.

I don't care much for the nickname. When I think of football monikers, I think of "Mean" Joe Green and "Bronko" Nagursky—not Plimpton, which doesn't have quite the ring of testosterone that I'm shooting for. I want a nickname that elicits lightning and Led Zeppelin, not pastels and daffodils. Understand, the Mariners are a tough, tattooed, heavily muscled brigade of barbarians, some of whom would make great prison movie extras. I'm trying to fit in. Being called Plimpton doesn't promote this agenda, and it doesn't assist me in putting on my game face. Every time Pudgie bellows "Plimpton," I want to break out in hysterics.

I'm not alone in my dream of playing football. Cezar, a former semi-pro soccer player from Romania, wants to make the Mariners as a kicker. At the end of one practice, Cezar boots balls through the goalposts as the team looks on, a ritual that Pudgie often uses to finish up on a light note. After each successful try, Pudgie orders Cezar to back up and kick from a greater distance. "Think that Romania is playing for the World Cup," yells Pudgie. "If your leg falls off, I'll sew it back on!" No doubt, Pudgie doesn't shy away from the theatrical. In fact, Pudgie had a small role in a Woody Allen movie, *Broadway Danny Rose*. (Unfortunately, his scene didn't make it into the film's final cut.) Now, Pudgie is so enthused by Cezar's success, his limp seems to disappear. As he hustles around with his slight hunch, Pudgie has to watch his every step because there's an obscured ditch or two or three somewhere on the field.

Cezar keeps connecting. "Hail Cezar!" yells Jonesy, the veteran Mariners tight end, after another Cezar make. Eventually Cezar lines up for a 50-yarder. Meanwhile, Pudgie does play-by-play. "We're playing the Marlboro Shamrocks!" Pudgie bellows, referring to the Mariners' arch rival, the league's defending champions, who hail from just outside Boston and seem to collect national championship trophies like baseball cards. In East Coast semi-pro ball, Brooklyn Mariners and Marlboro Shamrocks is the equivalent of Yankees and Red Sox, USC and UCLA, Michigan and Ohio State. "It's November 23, and there's seven seconds left. Some Irish cocksucker is trying to take your head off!" yells Pudgie.

Cezar misses.

As promising as Cezar is, Pudgie finds a kicker who is even stronger, a former college All-American out of nearby St. John's University. Before he tore his ACL, All-American was recruited by big-time powers such as Syracuse and the University of Virginia. Even now, he's still getting looks from the NFL. Just weeks ago, the Giants gave him an informal tryout. He often comes to practice with his father, a diminutive man who quietly lurks around the practice field. Some of the players refer to All-American's father as Garo Yepremian, the former Miami Dolphins kicker of Armenian descent, who was slow to pick up the customs of the game. Legend has it that when his coach informed him that their team lost the coin toss, Yepremian promptly ran to the center of the field and desperately tried to find the coin.

With the kicker position solidified, Pudgie turns his attention to other areas, specifically the quarterback slot. Just days before the season opener, Pudgie hits the recruiting trail, something that he revels and finds success in. Pudgie claims that he'll go into a ladies' room to find a decent ballplayer. Fortunately, everyone is spared this indignity because a New Jersey club folds, which is all too often the norm for fledgling semi-pro football squads. Pudgie snaps up the disbanded team's nucleus, including their quarterback, Jay, a Flutie-esque professional indoor league veteran who can throw a 75-yard spiral on the run. Jay played his college ball at SC—except it's *not* Southern Cal. Southern Connecticut provides a steady number of players for Pudgie.

Ultimately, the Brooklyn Mariners' roster is comprised of all-stars from New York City and its surrounding areas. I doubt that more than a quarter of the players are actually from Brooklyn. Throughout the pre-season, Pudgie attempts to keep us humble, as well as motivated, by dressing us down. "I've got more cheerleaders than football players!" Pudgie growls at one point. As he adds players, Pudgie cuts others, walking up to guys after practice, informing them that their services are no longer required. As the first game approaches, Pudgie refuses to commit to a definite roster, preferring to keep everyone on edge. "If you don't go to the game, that does not mean that you're *not* on the team," announces Pudgie after one pre-season practice. "If you go, that does not mean that you're *on* the team. That could be the last trip you ever take!"

A week later, we're off to Pennsylvania for the opener. On the bus, the guys have on fella flicks like *State of Grace* and Christopher Walken's *King of New York*. No one really watches. We've seen these movies a million times. Meanwhile, in the front, Pudgie counsels All-American on potential professional opportunities. By his own admission, Pudgie's forte is not strategy. Pudgie, whose playing experience is solely sandlot, brings enthusiasm to the table and makes the Mariners happen through sheer will. He gets the field, the zebras, the uniforms, and, most important, the talent, players he refers to as the Studs, "guys that show up and blow guys off the line of scrimmage because that's what they do." Consequently, the Mariners don't lose much. In 1991, they won the semi-pro national championship, and they seem to always be in contention for the title.

More than two hours later, we arrive just as the sun is going down. Spirits are high as we dress in the open, adjacent to the field. It's actually a rugby field, ironic because Johnny, Pudgie's son, is off at an important rugby tournament and won't be suiting up. In fact, many of Pudgie's Studs aren't present for tonight's game, which no one seems too concerned about. McGee, the longtime Mariners running back, one of the few Brooklyn natives on the team, is in the lineup and gets taped on a foldout table. Undersized with a crew cut, McGee toes around opponents with the grace of a ballerina and runs into them with the ferocity of a sledgehammer. While McGee is a punishing, violent force on the field, he is a calming influence off it. As the team's unofficial therapist, he's often encouraging backups and constantly counseling the irascible Pudgie. When Pudgie is red-faced and screaming at the tops of his lungs, which is quite often, McGee gently places his arm on the coach's back and massages him with soothing words. This early evening, McGee is concerned about Pudgie's excessive drinking, a conversation Pudgie wants no part of. "I drink red wine!" snaps Pudgie.

Meanwhile, I wage a quiet but vigilant war to put on my shoulder pads, specifically my straps. I want to ask someone for assistance but feel embarrassed. Finally, Cezar can't help but notice my futile struggle and comes over to assist. Unfortunately, the Romanian backup kicker is a less than ideal candidate. "I've never done this before," he says nervously as he attempts to hook me up. My straps aren't my only concern either. There's a shortage of helmets, and I have to scavenge the equipment pile for something, anything, to put on my head. I don't expect to play, but I at least want to look somewhat official. As far as playing time, Pudgie has granted me no guarantees, and I haven't asked for any. I want to be just another player. If I get in, it's because I earned it. Finally, I find a helmet, kind of. It looks like a relic from the 1970s. You might as well put a red flowerpot on my head. However, it'll have to do. I guess I'm semi-official, which is fitting because we're semi-pro, right? As I grab my flowerpot, I become self-conscious and hope that Pudgie didn't witness the earlier episode. I fear that I've become fodder for a Mariner Inn soliloquy. I can just see Pudgie gulping down copious amounts of red wine while recalling my pre-game difficulties.

Plimpton could barely get on his pants!

And then, he had to get the backup Romanian kicker to help him with his straps!

And then, Plimpton put a flowerpot on this head!

Red wine and guffaws for EVERYONE!

After months of preparation, we kick off. Bodies ram violently, pads crash. Before the first whistle, I realize that I've greatly underestimated the level of violence that takes place in semi-pro. I'm not the only one. "It looks so easy on television," Cezar tells me later. Pec, a longtime Mariners offensive lineman who always seems to look annoyed, is instantly disgusted with the new crop of Mariners talent. "No hitters," he declares flatly, shaking his head as he looks over the scattered bodies. Pec is hardcore. He wants to knock around as many people as possible, and he doesn't necessarily care who. Since rival Marlboro often plays on Sundays, Pec often plays for the Mariners on Friday or Saturday night and then drives up north to play for Marlboro.

As the game unfolds, we're in disarray, looking nothing like a team that'll make a national title run. We fumble twice. Jay throws two interceptions. All-American attempts a long field goal but the Moose malfunction. An opposing player shoots right up the middle, and the attempt is blocked. At the end of the first quarter, we're down 19–0 and the sideline contingent is downright maudlin. "I'm not going to practice on Wednesday," someone grumbles.

"I'm too old for this," grouses Pudgie solemnly, sounding as if he's about to announce his retirement at halftime. Just months ago, I heard that the New York City Fire Department's football squad forced Pudgie to step down from his post as head coach. This season, no doubt, Pudgie wants to make a statement, show the FDNY what they're missing. This debut, however, is only showing that his team is ill-prepared. A moment after Pudgie's implied retirement, he's back to frantically pacing the sideline, going absolutely ballistic. "If I see another helmet on the ground, I'll kick someone in the balls!" he roars.

I don't dare go near Pudgie, and I feel fortunate that I'm clutching my flowerpot—and that I'm wearing a cup.

In the second quarter, we fight back. West Virginia, a fierce middle linebacker, knocks the quarterback unconscious. The Tank, McGee's backfield mate who's only 5-foot-6, rumbles over men twice his size. "That's what I'm talkin' about!" Mariners bark as they stomp up and down the sidelines. "That's what I'm talkin' about!"

At the half, we have life, down by just 10, still very much in it. Behind the rugby goalposts, where we dressed, Pudgie addresses us. He's not acting like himself. He's actually quite calm. Win or lose, Pudgie tells us, we should keep our heads high, play clean, and leave the field like gentlemen, like Mariners. He then takes a long, deep swig of air and switches modes.

The placid demeanor was a smoke screen.

His raspy voice rises, more Pogues than Springsteen. His face contorts and turns practically as red as a Mariners jersey. In closing, he exhorts us to run the other team off the field. After the speech, I'm caught up in a Pudgie-induced hysteria and I approach Coach Rod, the special teams coach.

"If you put me in, I'll hit someone," I tell him.

"I'll consider it," says the retired firefighter as he studies his clipboard. I tried.

In the second half, we scratch to within 8 points, and it comes down to one last, final play on fourth and what seems like forever. Jay throws a stunning 50-yard spiral, hitting the receiver right on his fingertips.

After all this, we'll surely get the 6, tie the game with a 2-point conversion, and All-American will nail one in OT to win it. After all this, for Pudgie, we'll show the guys at the FDNY!

But it's not to be.

The receiver can't quite bring the ball in, and our euphoria switches to utter agony and disgust. "Right through his hands," Pudgie growls.

We're officially 0-1.

═════

On the ride back, I quickly fall asleep. Forgive me. Waiting and watching on the sidelines is exhausting. When we stop at a rest stop in the middle of nowhere, I wake up. "I'll negotiate," Pudgie says as he steps off the bus. Ten minutes later, Pudgie emerges with an enormous case of Budweiser. "I'm a sixty-six-year-old teenager," he mutters. The rest of the ride is anything but celebratory, though. I'm half asleep when I hear Pudgie lamenting the loss of one of his friends, a Mariner, I presume. "He was forty-two," recalls Pudgie. "He left eight children."

The following Wednesday at practice, the wide receiver can't escape the drop, mumbling to himself about the last-second play that he'll never get back. At the game, teammates had tried to console him. "Professionals do it all the time," they told him. Meanwhile, Pudgie focuses on our upcoming opponent, the New York Panthers, a tough team from the neighboring borough of Queens. In reality, every team is tough. You gotta be tough to play semi-pro.

Just before the half, we're up big, 19–0. With eleven seconds left, we have to kick off. We're a man down on the kick-off team, otherwise known as the suicide squad because this assignment requires players to run in the open field, making them vulnerable to hits from other players running with a full head of steam. Being on the suicide squad is akin to being a human pinball. In fact, Yepremian was ordered to exit the field immediately after he kicked off because of the danger involved. As I stand on the sidelines, I'm not considering any of this. I'm scheming on how to get in the game. Finally, I shuffle myself into position so that Coach Rod can spot me. After I get no response, I reluctantly, ever so slightly, raise my hand.

Finally, I get the nod.

If I somehow get to football heaven, I hope to see a who's who of greats in the big locker room in the sky. In one corner, Knute Rockne will be rallying the Four Horsemen. Walter Payton will be on a stool with his signature headband. Johnny U. will be quietly tossing a ball, perhaps looking over a playbook. There'll be plenty of others, names that I don't know but certainly should.

On this Friday night, right after Rambo yells "Full speed," I see none of this. I see a single light—and that's it.

When I finally come to, the Panther player who rammed his face mask into my chin when he blasted me is hovering over me, taunting me. I wish I could say that he was a juiced-up monster. My vision still blurry, but I manage to make out that he's about my size. I don't know where I am. I could use a stretcher. It's not in the budget.

It's halftime.

The field is empty, just the imperfect grass of Kings Bay under the lights. Johnny, Pudgie's good-natured son and a Mariners defensive back, offers a hand.

"You all right?" he asks.

I can make out his face—well, some of it.

"Yeah, I'm all right." I'm lying my ass off because I don't want to seem like I can't take a hit. Like a punch-drunk fighter, I struggle to stagger up.

Immediately, Johnny informs me that the hit was clean—not the news that I was looking for. If I'm gonna get laid out, I prefer that it be a cheap hit, so that I can serve as a rallying point for the guys.

As is, I'm just a scrub.

I walk back to the end zone, where the rest of the team is on one knee awaiting Pudgie's words of wisdom. Standing off to the side, I try to remain inconspicuous in the sea of uniforms and pretend like it's business as usual: *Yeah, I got hit, but it's all part of the game, and I've been hit before, and I'll be hit again and again and again. No biggie—I'm a ball player.*

Immediately, my facade is blown to pieces.

"Hey Plimpton?" someone yells. I don't have to look to see who it is. It's Rambo. If I hadn't been trying to impress him and kept my head on a swivel, rotating back and forth like a windshield wiper, I could've avoided this fiasco. Now, I have to face the consequences. I have to pay the bill for my hubris: I thought I could actually play with these guys.

"How's your brain?" Rambo shouts.

Everyone cracks up.

I'm completely rattled and embarrassed and a lot of other things. Fortunately, I have the bearings to figure out that I'm being tested yet again. On the field, I've already miserably failed my first test. My new test: Will I take the heat, the ribbing, and stay in the pocket? Or will I run away to the locker room, which is actually a walk-in, transportable Dumpster? As everyone enjoys a moment at my expense, I use every fiber of my being to stand tall and force a smile. Still dazed, I don't listen to Pudgie's halftime talk. Afterward, I walk back to the sidelines with Coach Rod.

"How far did I get down the field?" I ask him.

"Not far," Coach Rod says.

"What, 25 yards?"

"20."

I shake my head and return to the bench, where I remain on the sidelines with my helmet on, not because I expect to play, but because I'm hiding again. McGee, the team's unofficial therapist, tells me to take my helmet off, so I don't exacerbate my headache. As I rub the bump on my chin where the opposing player stuck his face mask, Rambo comes over. I'm not in the mood for his posturing, but I have nowhere to run. They're certainly not gonna allow me on the field again.

"You ever play this game before?" Rambo asks.

"No, not really," I tell Rambo.

I opt to not tell Rambo about playing in my cramped room as a kid. Back then, I kept going until my father threatened to call the cops. Later, my mother gave him grief for not sending me to the expensive therapist. After several threats of divorce, my father attempted a different, less confrontational approach. "We're not meant to be football players," my father told me. "We're just not built for that."

Rambo looks me directly in the eye. Even in full uniform, you can make out his powerful physique. He's not tall, but he makes the most of what little he has. He's just one big muscle. "You got more balls than half the pussies on this team!" Rambo declares before walking away.

═══════
═══════

The following week, we're on the road again just over the water in Hoboken, New Jersey, playing on a less than ideal playing surface. It's a concrete hard, artificial turf field in the middle of a number of construction projects. Also, the field doubles as a baseball diamond and second base is on the 40-yard line. In the stands, there are about eight people. I know. I counted them.

None of the guys seem too concerned about the opponent. As for myself, I've changed my focus. It has become all about making everyone forget that one play at the end of the half. Before the season, I aspired to be something like Russell Crowe's character in *Gladiator*. Now, Morgan Freeman's character in *The Shawshank Redemption* is a reach. Still, I just might get my shot at redemption on this very day, as many of Pudgie's Studs are AWOL, most conspicuously Jay. Not surprisingly, this lack of commitment infuriates Pudgie. All year, he works to put a season together, and now the Studs don't show. Pudgie seems genuinely hurt. In the back of the end zone, just in front of a construction site, Pudgie addresses us. He thanks us for coming and disparages the no-shows. "I'm sick of the Triple-A all-star bullshit!" he blares before mocking someone's excuse. "They got an Aunt Nellie in England who's having an operation, and they're waiting for a phone call!" A moment later, Pudgie tells us how he was considering forfeiting the game. Of course, that's not going to happen. Pudgie doesn't quit. In closing, Pudgie makes this dramatic declaration. "We'll dance with who we brung!"

And dance we do. The no-shows aren't a factor. All-American finds his form, booting a 47-yarder. Rambo finally takes a hand off and scores. "It was the first time in fourteen years," he barks out as he runs off the field. I can make out through his face mask that he's smiling, just barely. For weeks, Rambo's face has been locked in a perpetual scowl. Rambo's chagrined that he's not in the starting lineup, having been relegated to special teams. He was hoping to use this season as a showcase or even a warm-up for the XFL. Instead, Rambo's looking for a position, just like myself. We've both got something to prove.

Unfortunately, I don't quite know how I'm gonna prove it, because I've discovered I'm not as tough as I thought I was. After actually experiencing the game and getting lit up—torched, really—I'm terrified of getting back in. Actually, I'm intimidated just participating in the handshake line.

In jock parlance, I'm shook.

But somehow, I muster up the courage and volunteer my services to Coach Rod, who immediately rebuffs me. It's safe to say that I'm firmly on Coach Rod's shit list. As I understand it, Pudgie ripped him a new asshole after I got knocked out. In Pudgie's mind-set, Mariners are conquerors, the ones who are supposed to inflict their will and put other teams in wheelchairs, something Pudgie has actually stated in one of his raucous pre-season pep talks. Meanwhile, I've become fodder for another team's highlight reel—if they had highlight reels. After Coach Rod turns me down, I opt for Plan B: Rambo, who I figure has some pull. I ask him to make an appeal on my behalf. Rambo listens but agrees to nothing. As the minutes whittle away, Rambo runs off the field, directly toward me.

"Go in for me!" he orders gruffly.

"Did you tell Coach Rod?" I ask. I know that I must sound pathetic.

"Look, just go in for me," he blares with his signature psychotic look in his eyes. "I'm hurt!"

I'm skeptical. Rambo looks fine, and he doesn't get hurt. And if he was actually hurt, he wouldn't admit it. He's Rambo. As I stand on the sidelines, I find myself in a quandary: If I get on the field, I might get maimed. If I stay on the sidelines, Rambo might come after me.

After some serious contemplation, I decide to go for it and sneak into the game. I nervously shuffle into the mass of Mariners red helmets that are about to go on to the field and attempt to remain inconspicuous.

Yes, I'm hiding again.

As I wait, I visualize myself running down the field with my head on a swivel, giving a pop to an opposing player. I'm desperately trying to psyche myself up to actually do it and overcome my fears. As I visualize the cacophony of shoulder pads and helmets, I notice that Rambo is in the huddle as well. I count eleven players—plus myself. Apparently, Rambo has had a miracle recovery. Obviously, I can't go on the field. I can just envision the referee explaining the penalty: "Fifteen-yard penalty: eleven men on the field—plus Plimpton!" I fear that this act of insubordination just might push Pudgie over the edge. He might kick me off the team or in the groin, or both. Like a concerned parent chasing after his wandering toddler, Coach Rod directs me back to the far depths of the sidelines. By the end of the game, I'm practically standing with the eight fans.

———

My personal struggles aside, the season rolls along smoothly. The Moose blow people off the ball. The Studs go to town. McGee lays people out and then returns to the sidelines to give a pick-me-up to a discouraged backup or two. Besides the opening game, we haven't lost. Pudgie has his sights on Marlboro and more—much more. "I'm sixty-six years old!" Pudgie yells after another victory. "I might drop dead in December, but before they put me under, I want them to put another ring on my finger!"

Meanwhile, I don't play, and I don't practice, either. No one really practices, for that matter. As the season grinds along, practice becomes even less regimented, not to mention attended. Offense and defense go over a few formations, which I'm not a part of, and that's basically it. It doesn't really matter. The Mariners run the I, meaning they run on instinct. Having played so long, guys just know what to do. I, of course, don't know what I'm doing.

I can run, though.

After practice, I run sprints wearing my shoulder pads and helmet. I run with Sean, the captain of the defense, who has played various levels of professional ball. He's a diehard, veteran Mariner, one of the few who takes practice seriously. While all the guys just go with helmets and shoulder pads in practice, Sean, who plays linebacker and is also the team's punter, wears a full uniform. We run end zone to end zone, repeatedly. No headphones, just the steady soundtrack of exhale and our feet hitting the imperfect grass. As I sprint, I practice using my peripheral vision, so I can avoid getting blindsided again. I go until Sean stops. He won't let me quit.

It's good to get used to running around with equipment, but it's not enough. If I'm going to actually play in a game, I need something else. A boxer needs to get punched. I need to get blasted. I rescind Pudgie's "no hitting in practice" policy and ask a player, a special teams standout, to run into me a few times. He's not huge like many of the guys, but he was good enough to get some looks from a few big-time colleges. After practice, under the lights, we line up across from one another and run into each other several times. We're two bulls with no matador.

However, we have a coach who's leaning toward castration.

We're conducting this dubious exercise way off to the side, practically in the dark, so Pudgie can't witness it. It's 5 yards in the right direction, but it doesn't come close to vanquishing my demons. Unfortunately, I'm still shaken. Meanwhile, Rambo hazes me as if it's his job. "Do you wear pink underwear?" he asks. I have no comeback for that one. Actually, my comeback is getting into an actual game. I tell as much to Sean. "Your time will come," he promises.

It never does. I fall into a mellow malaise, doing what I do best: hanging out, enjoying the spectacle of the season from the safety of the sidelines, where I take in the grunts and grimaces as I drink a hot chocolate or two from the concession stand. Sometimes I hold the ball for Cezar, so he can practice kicks. Between series, West Virginia, the ferocious linebacker, checks in every once in a while. He has become a friend. He'd get me into a game, but he's a newcomer with his own frustrations. As one of the players from the folded Jersey outfit, he's just trying to solidify his spot. Unfortunately, for whatever reason, West Virginia never made it to Morgantown. Shit happens. Then, his semi-pro team in Jersey folded. Now, his hair is starting to go, but he's still inspired to torpedo opposing team's quarterbacks. During breaks in the action, he seeks me out to lay out his screenplay's plot. Like myself, it's a work in progress.

After yet another win and victory celebration at the Mariner Inn, I ponder the unthinkable: throwing in the towel, quitting. However, this plan is swiftly met with strong opposition from Sean. "I'll never talk to you again," promises Sean, one of the few guys on the team that knows my actual name. We never talk in the first place, I think to myself, but I hold my tongue. Why does my quitting bother Sean so much? People probably tell Sean to quit all the time, that he's playing a young man's game for no money and, well, no nothing. It's not like the papers care about the Mariners. Trust me, I'm the team's press representative. People probably say this: Why don't you just quit while you can still walk? Well, simply, Sean won't quit because football is what he does. Quitting is not in his playbook. He loves the game so much that he traveled to Switzerland to play it professionally. Sean won't accept quitting from himself, and he won't accept it from me. I can't let Sean or myself down, so I keep showing up. Along the way, I rationalize my position. Not everyone gets to play. There are all kinds of roles on a team. Some guy deals with the equipment. Someone carries the water. And sometimes, someone is just a persona.

While I don't contribute on the field (or maybe I do in *very* intangible ways), I do partake in the post-game celebrations at the Mariner Inn, where it's dark but we're lit, and not necessarily from the alcohol. Everyone's still intoxicated from the game. At the Inn, there are no women and not much conversation. The Caddie guards the jukebox, which blares Springsteen. Rousing yet melancholy, it's a fitting selection. Rambo boasts about being one of the "last gladiators." On a rare occasion, Pudgie has been known to do a little jig. Mostly, though, these are stoic affairs, and we communicate with our eyes. Often, a lot of guys get obliterated. Mariners like their spirits, sometimes to their detriment. According to a few of the guys, some of the team got loaded the night before a national championship game, which they consequently lost. Hey, they were on vacation, paying their own way. They can do as they please. At one point, a radio host complains that Pudgie seemed slightly inebriated during an interview. Pudgie's perceived intoxicated state didn't surprise me in the least. However, the fact that it was before nine in the morning on a Tuesday did.

One night after a game, I'm at the bar with Billy, a linebacker and one of the team's leaders. When Billy comes off the field after making a big stop, he's an unforgettable sight. He mimics the Frankenstein monster's walk and flexes like the Hulk, his face twitching as if he's been struck by lightning. This evening, he's sitting on a stool, feeding me some kind of strange gin concoction. "Plimpton," Billy says slowly, looking me dead in the eye. Then he stirs his drink and tilts his head down, before popping back up. "Plimpton," he repeats, locking eyes with me again. As we imbibe, I consider worst-case scenarios as far as where this evening can possibly go. I don't want to pass out. Actually, I can't pass out. If I do, I might wind up the casualty of a practical joke, a rite of passage for a rookie. I imagine passing out and waking up in the Mariner Inn's men's room naked, covered in black magic marker.

With the exception of one word, I'm completely bare. I can't make it out. Then it comes into focus.

It says PLIMPTON.

"Plimpton," repeats Billy, returning me to the dark bar. Billy likes the way it sounds, just like Pudgie and the rest of the guys. Personally, I think it sounds a little too much like, well, pimple. Come to think of it, though, that's exactly what I am. I'm a pimple. I won't go away and my game isn't much to look at. How do I put this? I'm just *there*.

Whether I like it or not, my moniker has taken on a life of its own. There's even a guy on the Mariners message board who refers to himself as Plimpton. On the positive side, I've become something of a nexus for this team, which is rarely together. Many of the players may not know one another, but they know my nickname. While I never wanted to be Plimpton, I surrender to it, begrudgingly. When Sean introduces me to his girlfriend, one of the few women to enter the male sanctum of the Inn, I hold out my hand. "I'm Plimpton," I tell her.

For the record, I am completely sober.

Despite my nickname's unifying powers, we're on the brink of unraveling as we roll through the season. We're bored with our opponents, so we have to come up with a worthy one: ourselves. Inexplicably, All-American misses field goals and even some extra points. Pec looks like he's about to devour him as if he's a plate of fried mozzarella sticks. Despite McGee's best therapeutic efforts, one of the backup running backs stops showing up. Uncharacteristically, Jay is forcing the ball. He's frustrated with himself and probably the outspoken Pec, who attempts to control the huddle and makes the bold claim that the Mariners are "his team." Jay's not the only one unnerved by the outspoken lineman. Throughout the season, Pudgie and Pec repeatedly bicker. "I'm the coach!" Pudgie reminds Pec a time or two. At one point, Pudgie mutters that no other player has ever given him as much trouble. No doubt, Pudgie and Pec love one another.

They just can't live with each other.

As personalities clash, our differences become apparent. While the team is predominantly white, Jay and some of the other Mariners are black. As the team wins ugly, there are rumblings that a racial slur was uttered toward Jay. I didn't hear it, but I heard a few of the guys refer to it, and I saw the usually calm and collected Jay walk away extremely agitated at one point. Jay and I share an unspoken understanding: he understands a dream, mine as well as his own. While I just want to play a few snaps, Jay wants to get back to playing in arenas. I'm surprised that race has become an issue, but I shouldn't be. On the field, all kinds of boundaries are crossed. It's "violence that's legal," explains Rambo. If the slur was uttered, I believe that jealousy is the main culprit. Jay's the ultra-talented quarterback, the conductor. If he had another six inches, he probably would have wound up at *that* SC. Everything revolves around him. Frankly, some players resent that. When Jay starts faltering, he becomes vulnerable to barbs, however ignorant. With the Mariners, everyone's accountable. Success is expected. When it doesn't happen, guys start going after one another. Somehow, Pudgie resolves the issue and attempts to unify the team for the season's final stretch. "I'm the one who should be frustrated," Pudgie explains to us after a practice, holding his arms out as if he's asking for a life preserver. "I'm the only one that doesn't get to hit anyone!"

═══

For one of the last games of the season, I invite my friend Polo along. Before I knew him, Polo was a bookie, and that's the nickname the old-school wise guys gave him, because he always wore a polo shirt, usually red or blue. Sunday nights, Polo often takes me to some overpriced beef palace from his bookie days (think *GoodFellas* light), where he enjoys listening to me recount my football adventures, particularly the play in which I got knocked out. Every time we hang out, he asks to hear about it, and I don't disappoint.

"Full speed!" I mimic Rambo, slamming the table with both hands.

"You were knocked out?" Polo asks for something like the hundredth time, as he digs into what looks like half a cow.

"Like a light," I say, snapping my fingers.

When I'm done, Polo tilts his head, smiles, flexing his dimples, and always says the same thing. "You got balls!"

He raises a glass and toasts me—but not too much. It's water. A workout fiend, Polo's watching his figure. We have some laughs but I'm stuck on this: *If everyone says I have balls, why do I feel like a pussy?*

During the course of the season, Polo and I wind up having some epic man dates, going on awesome dinners followed by long walks. Inevitably, Polo always questions me on why my alma mater doesn't have a higher *U.S. News and World Report* rating. Polo has been an academia snob ever since he recruited a Harvard graduate into his bookie operation. After giving up bookmaking, Polo started listening to National Public Radio, attending performances at the Metropolitan Opera, and going on vacation to hang out at museums. He also enrolled at Columbia, which awarded him some sort of certificate. Polo considers this completely unacceptable, and he's in the midst of lobbying for an actual degree. Now, Polo constantly checks his phone as if the dean is going to deliver the diploma verdict at any moment. Once or twice, we go to a Columbia football game. However, I suspect that Polo isn't there to actually see the game. In all likelihood, he just wants to get some face time with esteemed faculty members.

During warm-ups before a Mariners game, Polo stands on the field. He's squared up, facing the action, pointing out which guys are on the juice, something I haven't given much thought to. I've got enough on my plate, and it seems to happen in just about every gym in America, so it probably happens here, too. If the players do it, they keep it quiet. There might be at least one player that takes stimulants, though. After one game, while walking back to the makeshift locker room to change, the player in question heard me yawn, and promptly suggested that I take some stuff that would keep me hyper-focused. Moments later, he opened up his hands, revealing a few pills. Though for all I know, it was Tylenol, and he was just having fun with me.

Longingly, Polo's gazing at the dewy Kings Bay grass, his expression clearly saying, *Hey, I'm the tough guy here.* He is indeed tough, well versed in taking sit-downs with street guys, armed only with his polo emblem. With Polo in the stands, I'm optimistic that today is my day. I actually expect to see time. As the game winds down, though, I'm still on the bench, feeling even more dejected than usual. Unfortunately, I've brought a witness to watch me sit. With a few minutes left, I take off my pads and slink to the walk-in Dumpster to change. Meanwhile, unbeknown to me, All-American has taken up my plight, asking Pudgie to insert me in the game. Halfway to the locker room, All-American shouts for me to return to the sidelines. As I jog back, I simultaneously attempt to put my thigh pads back in my pants. In the midst of this mad scramble, I notice that Pudgie and the All-American are smiling, which strikes me as unusual. With everyone focusing on the march to Marlboro, there have been few laughs this season. Most of the Mariners are past their prime playing days, and there might not be too many chances left. At every opportunity, Pudgie drills this point home by reminding us of his age. "I'm sixty-six years old!" he constantly grumbles. Before I can get all my gear on, time expires.

> Perhaps one play was more embarrassing in the history of the game: Yepremian's blocked field goal in Super Bowl VII. During this unforgettable play, Yepremian picked up the ball after his kick was blocked and threw an interception that was then returned for a touchdown. The significant difference between the plays, of course, was that Yepremian was actually on the field.

After the game, Polo and I don't partake in the post-game festivities. We ride back in silence. My ignominious sideline performance put a final nail in the coffin of our bromance. Years later, during one of our sporadic conversations, Polo has only fond memories of our friendship. "You were my best friend—for three months," Polo says. We always both laugh.

But I'm also a little sad.

─────

Having hit a new low, I'm resigned to sit out the rest of the season. I gave it a shot but was out of my league. No one will know about this embarrassing season except Polo and everyone he tells. Fortunately, Polo has no attention span. He's on to the next thing. I envisioned and manufactured this adventure. I can make it go away, forget it ever happened.

Except that I can't.

I'll never forget that I was one and done. So as I'm doing what I do, hanging out, I get something that a running back lives for: daylight. Pudgie is away at a wedding, no doubt downing a bottomless glass of red wine, and we're up by a pair of touchdowns. As the seconds tick off the clock, I make a decision: I can't hide anymore. I chuck the hot chocolate, get off the bench, and approach the defensive coach, who's standing in for Pudgie.

"Is there a chance that I can get in the game?" I ask politely, very politely. "I'd really appreciate it." I'm practically pleading. My entire existence I've been avoiding being that guy, the guy who has to ask to get in the game. I never wanted to be that guy.

No one wants to be that guy.

As I wait for the coach's response, I brace myself for the worst. My helmet's not even on. I don't deserve to be on the field. I don't deserve to be on the sidelines. Even with my shoulder pads on, you can make out that my shoulders are slumping. Slowly, the coach turns his head to the side, toward the field, and smiles.

"Sure," he says finally. "Go ahead."

Ready or not, it's my time. I put on my helmet and run onto the field. When I get to the huddle, West Virginia welcomes me, obviously surprised and understandably concerned.

"You're in?" he yells.

"I'm in!" I yell right back.

We're both behaving as if it's the Super Bowl. For me, it is.

After waiting a moment to confirm that security isn't looking to eject me like a mid-game streaker, West Virginia accepts my answer.

"Don't lock up!" West Virginia orders. "Don't lock up!"

He wants me to avoid an impossible-to-win sumo match with one of the opposing team's mammoth offensive linemen. Inside the Mariners huddle, I fight back the urge to smile and acknowledge everyone. Inside the stone-faced huddle, it's quiet, businesslike. We're closing out a game. That's what Mariners do. I'm enjoying the moment but can't let it overwhelm me as I did previously. I find an inner calm. When the huddle breaks, West Virginia points me to a spot. I get in my 3-point stance on the line of scrimmage across from the opposing team. Yes, they're quite large and imposing, and no, they don't know that my nickname is Plimpton. I try my best to ignore all of this, as well as their quarterback, who's calling out signals. I focus on the ball, just waiting for it to move even a hair. Then, I'll go. Finally, after an eternity, the ball is snapped. I explode left. Surprisingly, I find only open space, enough room for a small garden. Everything is in slow motion. Amid the bombardment of bodies, I spot the golden goose. I have a clear shot at the quarterback, who's preparing to throw. I make my final charge. I'm gonna get the ball . . . Just about there . . .

And then I'm not.

At the last moment, someone pushes me from behind, and I fall to the ground. Meanwhile, the quarterback throws it. We intercept. Somewhat disoriented, I manage to get up and run in the opposite direction with my head on a swivel, looking left, looking right, looking to pop someone.

OK, I just want to get off the field in one piece.

Finally, the play ends. Game over. I run off the field—and act like I've been there before. The defensive coach smiles widely and shakes my hand as I come off. For the season, I'm batting .500. I'll take it. Back at the Inn, I'm more upbeat than usual. Pec's mood remains dour. "What's with the in-line skating?" he scowls at me as if I just asked him to exchange Key lime pie recipes. That's just Pec making conversation, referring to my ritual of in-line skating to practice.

———

After running the table in the playoffs as expected, the season comes down to longtime Mariners nemesis Marlboro. It's always Marlboro. They've had the Mariners number the last few years. They have their own herd of Studs and Moose. They have the belt. We're merely the challenger. With the main event scheduled for Sunday evening, many of the Mariners drive up the night before.

Yes, we're playing on Sunday. We might never make it to the NFL, but we're finally going to play on Sunday.

Sunday afternoon, I depart on the team bus. The four-and-a-half-hour ride is practically silent. No movies. No card games. Rambo huddles in the back, smiling. He genuinely enjoys the long ride before the battle. In the middle of the bus, All-American wistfully recalls his Virginia recruiting visit. Mostly, though, we just sit and wait. Up front, Pudgie is uncharacteristically silent, staring intently out the window. I imagine that Pudgie is thinking what everyone else is thinking: How many more chances are we gonna get at Marlboro?

When we arrive in the small town just outside of Boston, it's drizzling. "We always get bad weather up here," grumbles one of the Mariners coaches. Despite the poor weather, the bleachers are packed with maybe four hundred vocal spectators. Under the lights, it feels like forty thousand. It's by far the largest crowd we've played in front of this season. I have one fan who has come to see me nervously fidget on the sidelines. I greatly appreciate her support. It's easy to support the starting quarterback. It takes a different breed to stand behind the scrub. These women are underappreciated, and I salute them!

Before the game, Pudgie is restrained. "Have fun out there," he orders. "Keep your head in the game." By now, I know what Pudgie is truly saying: *Knock someone on their ass and get the W!*

As I make my way to the sidelines, I notice a few players I haven't seen all season. I conclude that these are Pudgie's secret weapons: Super Studs. He's not taking any chances. This is it!

On the Mariners' very first possession, though, we're completely out of sync. We fumble and Marlboro recovers, and scores. The agonizing anxiety that enveloped the sidelines during the first game in Pennsylvania returns, except more potent this time. "Not Marlboro, not again," a player utters.

But we stay in the game. At the half, the contest is 7-7. When we run past the Marlboro bleachers, a few rowdies heckle us. Usually, I despise hecklers. They're bullies. However, I like these hecklers. Since they're putting their time and energy into me, I must be worth something. Like professionals, not semi-professionals, we run past them without incident and funnel into the visiting team's locker room, which is of course another converted walk-in Dumpster. It's kind of fitting that we always seem to be in these Dumpsters. Everyone on this team has been dumped in one form or another, told they're not good enough. Somehow, we always find a way to recycle ourselves and keep showing up. At some point, we've all had to ask to get in the game. Now, in the narrow confines of this makeshift locker room, the team that's never together is sitting shoulder to shoulder, face to face. I feel like a paratrooper preparing for a jump. In the narrow strip between the two rows of players, Pudgie slowly walks up and down, not uttering a word. I've never seen Pudgie this intense. With his mature eyes, the ones that have seen thousands of games, he attempts to look into our souls and deliver this message: *Guys, give this old but youthful-in-spirit coach this victory.*

You can do this! Ironically, with this silent pep talk, Pudgie's at his most compelling.

Of course, Pudgie doesn't leave it at that.

He makes his way to the front and pauses for us to listen. We hear absolutely nothing, just silence, which to Pudgie sounds sweeter than the melodic groan of bagpipes on St. Paddy's. No doubt, Marlboro is concerned, on the ropes. "They're shittin' all over themselves!" Pudgie finally unleashes, punching his fist in the air. "In the second half, we're gonna rub it all over their faces!"

"Yeah!" everyone shouts.

I'm convinced that we're gonna win this. We're gonna beat Marlboro—finally. Into the fourth quarter, the game remains deadlocked, and we're driving, on Marlboro's 8-yard line. It's going to happen. The red wine will flow!

Then we fumble, and Marlboro marches down the field and scores. Marlboro scores again, putting us down by two touchdowns with only four minutes remaining. It's just about over. With shifty Jay at the helm, there's always hope, though. Running the hurry-up, no-huddle offense, Jay gets a quick score. When he comes off the field, Jay, the Moose, and the Studs keep their helmets on. If we can recover the on-side kick, we'll get another shot. All-American certainly has the skill.

As he's supposed to, All-American keeps it on the ground. Unfortunately, everyone helplessly watches the football sputter out of bounds just in front of us, less than 10 yards from where he kicked it. Game over. Marlboro wins 24-17. No one should be surprised about the play's failure. I don't recall practicing it, not once. That's the nature of semi-pro ball. There's hardly enough time to practice extra points, much less specialty plays. Our season is over and we're despondent. "I'm never coming up here again," someone mutters.

Minutes after the game, the bus is back on the road. It's a school night. Yodels are passed out. Pudgie pushes his gallows humor, joking about his medical condition. No one's laughing. A collection goes around to pay for the bus, and guys throw in what they can. We stop at Burger King and eat on the bus. Eventually, I drift off. Somewhere in Connecticut, the bus stops to drop off the upstate contingent. The Caddie hits me on the shoulder and offers me a ride, so I grab my stuff. I share a passing glance with Pudgie. His eyes are wet, but he's not crying. There's no time for that. Before he goes under, there's that matter of getting another ring on his finger. Outside the bus, Billy, my drinking partner, along with Rambo and Ed, the equipment manager who got half his foot shot off in Vietnam, stand around silently in the brisk air. Billy eyes me steadily. Finally, unexpectedly, he throws an arm around me like an elephant tusk and we embrace, albeit awkwardly. This loss hurts. When we break, I trade glances with Rambo but nothing else. He did what we'd both want: he left his best talking out on the field. Another thing Rambo and I share: we're not much for good-byes. As I walk away, it's settling in that there won't be any more late-starting, unregimented practices and that the schedule is empty, which is exactly how I feel. . . . Right before I get into the Caddie's car, Ed yells over to me. I probably forgot something on the bus.

"What's up?"

"I'll see you next year," he asks, smiling. "Right?"

2
Welcome to the Major Leagues

Before a rare weekday matinee in September against the rival, second-place Orioles, a veteran colleague approaches and prepares me for a potential ambush. It's humid, the sun is scorching down, and it seems as if everyone is tanked. It's been eighteen years since the Yankees last won a world championship and the Bleacher Creatures, Yankee Stadium's rowdiest of rowdies, smell blood.

Me, I'm selling wienies.

"If you got a can opener, use it," a fellow vendor advises as we stand in line waiting for the franks to be dumped into our sturdy aluminum bins. "You might have to pull some eyes out." I'm nervous. Right out of the tunnel, the sun hits me in the eyes, and I break into my routine, succinct pitch. "Hot dogs hereyah!" I bark, attempting to match the crowd's intensity. I want to walk up the stairs but can't. Up a few flights, conspicuously right in the middle of the aisle, a ragged, middle-aged man desperately wants my attention. Already, he has everyone else's. He rocks his hips back and forth and grabs his crotch. "I've got a hot dog hereyah!" he slurs. "I've got a hot dog hereyah!" he repeats, even louder, just to make sure that I heard him. He's absolutely obliterated, and he clearly wants a showdown with Wienie Man.

OK, you want a showdown with Wienie Man, I'll give you a showdown.
Welcome to the Major Leagues.

——

It started with an assignment. It wasn't just *any* assignment. It was for a new magazine that promised real money. (In general, small newspapers, which I had been working for previously, pay transportation, if that.) But there was a catch: the Mag wanted me to work *undercover*—as a vendor. I was psyched. I wasn't in the best of spirits since I left my steady but very low-paying job at the paper, and this was a second chance. Even though I wasn't built for covering community board meetings and writing advertorials, the paper had kept me busy. This assignment was a challenge, plus it emancipated me from my desk, not to mention the confines of my shoebox of an apartment. It placed me firmly in the House That Ruth Built. If everything went according to plan, my work would appear in a real publication—OK a semi-real publication. As a start-up, the Mag was in the midst of getting funding, but the template made its prospects look awful good.

Though I didn't know much about the gig, I was ready to hawk. Besides watching the vendors during halftime of Jets football games at Shea Stadium as a kid, I hadn't given them much thought. Now, as I focused on this new possibility, I was intrigued. Could I become one of them?

———

Almost immediately, I went to work, putting in a call to Volume Services, the company that ran Yankee Stadium's concessions. They gave me a day and time and told me to show up for an interview at the stadium. When I arrive weeks later, I'm escorted to the stadium's basement with about thirty other hopefuls. There are empty tables throughout the room. I take a seat and wait. No one's too excited. Then again, it's 1996. Back then, the Yankees hadn't won a pennant in eighteen years. Yankee captain Derek Jeter was just starting his career. Whereas now the Yankees play to full houses nightly, the old Yankee Stadium felt like a ghost town.

I hand in my application to my interviewer, a Tony Danza look-alike in a blue-hooded sweatshirt with a full frontal zipper, who sits across from me at one of the tables. As we converse, other applicants are being interviewed simultaneously. I recall my final meeting a few months earlier with my former employer, the paper's publisher. "I'm giving you two weeks' notice," he told me abruptly. I wasn't surprised. I had seen it coming. Every week, the publisher had groused about the rising cost of paper. Any hint of a misstep, he was all over me. When I had the audacity to ask for a raise, he turned me down flat. My dismissal was inevitable. I had become expendable. "You'll qualify for unemployment benefits," he finally told me during our last conversation. "You've got *potential*. Good luck."

Don't let the door hit you on your way out.

Now, Tony's studying my application. Somewhat anxious, I abruptly break the awkward silence. "I want to be part of the baseball experience," I tell him. Tony nods politely as he confirms that I hadn't written my name in the address space, and that I didn't display any Ted Bundy tendencies. I leave three references. "They ain't callin' no one," a fellow applicant blurts out, just outside the stadium, waving her finger like a *Jerry Springer Show* audience member.

Fortunately, they did call. Weeks later, I'm one of about twenty-five rookies who show up at the stadium for orientation. We're an eclectic crew, representing every imaginable creed and color. We tour the legendary grounds. In the first few rows of the upper deck, we stand in silent awe as we examine the seemingly endless vacant rows of blue seats and the immaculately groomed field. Beyond the outfield wall, the 6 subway train is going by. It's a majestic, unforgettable site.

Unbeknown to my fellow colleagues, I'm on assignment, albeit by the skin of my teeth. Understandably, I'm not the Mag's first choice. Fortunately, none of my colleagues wanted the vendor assignment, and I was ready and willing, qualities that had served me well in the past. That's how I got to be my high school's backup soccer goalie. That's how I got the rugby beat for my college paper. I had learned this lesson repeatedly: when there's no position available, create your own. A senior editor at the Mag, Felix, finally got around to calling me about the vendor assignment. "Can you do it?" he asked impatiently. He'd probably already reached out and been turned down by a healthy roster of reporters. Felix had other matters to deal with. I had never met Felix, and he didn't want to meet me. I was the low guy on the totem pole, someone who would take the assignment and report. As Felix waited for my reply, I considered my prospects. Besides a writing assignment here and there, I was picking up whatever work, anything from market research to catering gigs. "I'll do it," I told Felix.

I was in the Major Leagues—of journalism.

During orientation, my vendor brethren and I meet the vendor com-
mander in chief, who has the tone of an intimidating drill sergeant.
Built like Joe Girardi, she lays down the law: Hustle hard except during the national anthem, at which time you stand at attention. Do
not run into (or over) patrons, throw merchandise (Cracker Jacks or
peanuts), or keep foul balls, and don't sell in the corridors (passage-
ways in the interior of the stadium). Also, appearance must be con-
servative. Long or dyed hair and piercings are absolutely forbidden.
George Steinbrenner, the team's owner who was dubbed the Boss by
the newspaper tabloids, was uptight and on top of *everything*, including vendor appearance. Before games, the Boss was known to inves-
tigate the premises, searching out imperfections such as unshaven
vendors.

On my first day, I report to the bowels of Yankee Stadium two hours
before first pitch, as vendors are required to do before every game. This
allows the hawker higher-ups enough time to assess how many vendors
are present and where they should be assigned. The basement's odor is
unforgettable: the smell of ancient ketchup. I'm directed to the rookie
vendor locker room, a low-ceilinged, drab closet with high school–style
lockers, where I change into my uniform of heavily starched white pants
and a blue jersey. Moments later, I *am* the Good Humor Man. As I wait
in the corridor, I can't ignore the funky aroma of vendor dinner. It smells
like last week's beans and franks. The veterans—men who sell beer, the
most coveted item—quietly sit against the wall talking among themselves. This is a closed club, and the beer vendors don't acknowledge
anyone who isn't in their crew.

Meanwhile, I manage to overhear the conversation between a set of
twins, two dark-haired, diminutive men wearing glasses. "I hope they
give me ice cream," one chirps to the other. "I really want ice cream. Why
won't they give me ice cream?" *What's so special about ice cream?* Later,
I learn that ice cream is light and extremely popular with kids. It's often
purchased in bunches because kids travel in packs. Since it's arguably the
lightest item, it often goes to women, who make up a minuscule percent-
age of the vendor workforce.

I wind up making small talk with a brawny construction worker, Big
Papi, who's returning to vending after a three-year sabbatical. Like my-

self, he's shifting his feet. "I'm a little nervous," Big Papi confides, avoiding eye contact. "I don't know why."

Forty minutes before first pitch, the mass of blue-and-white-clad vendors swarm toward the end of a tunnel. A tall, lean man with a bulldog voice and glasses booms out assignments, which are decided by seniority. Veteran vendors get the best items (beer) and make about 18 percent commission, plus tips. Rookies like myself start at 13 percent commission and get less popular items, such as soda on a chilly night. (Later, I learn that if I work about two-thirds of the games, my commission will be upgraded the following season.) Neophytes sell the worst items in the worst places, ice cream at night in April, just about anything in the sparsely populated mezzanine, or worst of all, the dreaded All Sport drink, a Gatorade knock-off, which I dub the Green Monster because it's heavy and tough to sell. (Among vendors, the rumor is that the Boss owns a piece of All Sport.) Few first-time vendors return to the stadium after a night lugging around the Monster. On the other hand, old-timers, some of whom have worked at the stadium for decades, sell beer, which can net as much as $500 on a very good night. Another popular item is peanuts. They're light, and because they cost $3.50, customers will often allow the vendor to keep the change. A hundred sales selling nuts, you do the math. However, there's a downside to nuts: some fans request that their nuts be thrown to them, but throwing nuts is absolutely forbidden because it's a lawsuit waiting to happen.

For my debut, I get Yankee souvenir plastic cups filled with cola in the left-field upper deck, no easy task, considering the tray of twelve mammoth sodas isn't light, the soda isn't cheap, and we're definitely *not* in the throes of a heat wave. Most daunting, the steep, narrow steps of the upper deck rival the Himalayas. I absolutely refuse to look down at the field, keeping my eyes focused on the steps that are directly in front of me. As I slowly descend the stairs one step at a time, I feel as if I'm one false move away from having my tray fall on outfielder Darryl Strawberry, who's in the midst of a comeback. I can't watch Straw patrol the outfield because I have to concentrate on not falling down the stairs. As I avoid legs that spill out from the seats and into my walking space, the newsman in me can't help but envision the next day's *New York Post* headline if my balance betrays me: Soda Man Bombs Straw Man.

Despite the physical strain, I pitch my product with a vengeance and, to my surprise, people actually buy from me. Money aside, I push for sales so the tray will become lighter. "Souveneeyah sodah hereyah! Getcha soda hereyah!" Shouting is cathartic. I'm no natural, but I can do this gig. After getting canned, I'm getting my confidence back—one stair and sale at a time. Eager kids surround my tray and wave dollar bills in my face. Fans bounce into me and don't apologize. When you're a vendor, you're part of the furniture. "Welcome to the Bronx," says a young cotton candy vendor. After a few innings, I've worked up a good sweat and my voice is hoarse.

There are several vendor-reloading areas—commissaries—throughout the stadium. I refer to them as Pits, narrow, tense virtual saunas where vendors pay, reload product, vent, and rehydrate, the latter of which can be tricky. When there are no spare Styrofoam cups (or "courtesy cups") available, which is often, dehydrated vendors gulp cola—the only drink available—from the cups reserved for customers. In short, customer cups equal cash. I repeat, customer cups equal cash. If a customer cup is missing, management assumes that a cup of soda was sold or stolen. So after drinking out of the customer cups, vendors return them to the cup supply area and mix them with the untouched cups. How many customers drank out of cups that were first used by vendors? Damn good question.

By the seventh inning, it's vendor quitting time, and I return to the rookie locker room, which is slowly growing on me. Everyone is still hyped from the game, and perhaps all the caffeine. I peel off my sweaty uniform and throw it in the humongous hamper. I change back into my street clothes, having made $53, weary but exhilarated. I will sleep well tonight, and I won't be working out tomorrow morning. Actually, I *can't* work out. Vending is exhausting.

After the first night, Big Papi goes AWOL. There's no shortage of vendors, though, who run the gamut from civil servants to actors to teachers to accountants—lots of accountants. Vending is their part-time gig. When the Yankees are out of town, some of the vendors hawk at nearby Shea Stadium in Flushing, Queens, which has a reputation with some of the Yankee vendors as being somewhat of a hawker boot camp because it has stricter rules.

Beer vendor Ric Goldfarb, a.k.a. "Cousin Brewski," who works as an accountant, is the stadium's most well-known vendor. He has passed out pins ("Get a buzz from the cuz") to his loyal clientele and has appeared on local radio, showcasing his Catskills-style humor. Brewski quips that vendors have a low divorce rate because they're too busy working to spend time arguing with their spouses.

Within the vending ranks, there's no shortage of colorful characters. One is nicknamed Baltimore because he commutes from there for games. Baltimore also works games in Philadelphia and Atlanta, and aspires to hawk at the Super Bowl. (Inexplicably, it doesn't appear as if Baltimore vends for his hometown Orioles.) Often, Baltimore performs play-by-play in the locker room, oblivious to the fact that he's ignored. Another famous character is known as the Rabbi. He claims to be an actual rabbi, albeit one without a congregation, and he's painfully methodical when he makes change, to the chagrin of many a fan. Another vendor is known for touching himself in inappropriate places before serving his hot dogs. I have never met this individual—and I really don't want to.

For the most part, I don't communicate much with my vending brethren, as hawking is a solitary endeavor. Plus I'm a rookie. Most of the veterans figure that rookies will succumb to poor sales and disappear. Charlie Hustle is the exception, though. I'm not sure if Charlie Hustle told me his name, which wouldn't be too unusual, as many of the vendors remain nameless to one another. Vendors know each other's faces and what item they hawk and if they can move it or not. For instance, when a vendor sees me, he might say something like this: *The rookie's got soda in the uppers, if he's lucky. If he's unlucky, he might get stuck with All Sport.* Hustle's talkative, though, and we strike up a conversation. A Bronx native, Hustle is a lifer. That's the vendor term for guys who *live* for the gig and will not leave the job unless they're fired or expire.

On occasion, when Hustle hawks dogs, I trail him with my soda tray, so customers will have the opportunity to have a drink with their dog. Customer service isn't my sole purpose. I enjoy watching Hustle work. He's quick like a cat. Like Pete Rose, he hustles as if his life depends on it. Like the real Charlie Hustle, he also takes chances that could cost him his job. He nags customers for tips, sells in the corridors, and works every angle imaginable. Before games, he hangs out in Monument Park, where there are plaques and tributes to retired Yankee greats, and takes photos of fans (with their cameras) in hopes of getting a generous gratuity for his trouble.

One day before a game, Hustle pulls me aside and fills me in on the dark side of vending. "There's lots of scams around here," he says matter-of-factly. One particularly odious trick: retrieving used beer cups off the ground, getting them refilled from one of the concession counters in the stadium's corridor, and then reselling them. This is basically a cash cow because the vendor will pocket the total sale. Certainly, Hustle isn't the only one *working* it. As I learn later, theft is an accepted part of Yankee Stadium vendor culture. "If you wanna make money," explains a burly pit foreman to me after a game, "you gotta cheat!"

I play it straight and sell hard. I genuinely enjoy vending. Perhaps it's the physicality, or the tangential connection to professional sports. At a very small gathering I'm fortunate enough to be introduced to a famous sportswriter, a regular guest on ESPN, someone who practically makes a living off ridiculing a particular star player's perceived aloof attitude. When I proudly tell him that I'm a vendor, I expect the well-known television personality to be curious, just a little. Everyone else seems to have questions about vending. Instead, to my surprise, ESPN is completely disinterested—and very aloof. He couldn't care less.

———

I convince my pal, Doc, an actor-playwright, to get a job as a counter worker, which pays a straight, hourly wage. Doc is a unique individual. He works out like a fanatic and talks like Lebowski. We had bonded over grind-it-out market research work, which would often involve approaching strangers and asking them survey questions. Doc refers to us as the A Team.

No one else refers to us as the A Team.

With his excellent oratory skills, Doc reads a nice survey. And when he reads it, he closes in on the target, often getting right in their wheelhouse, close enough so that they can often taste *his* lunch. Sometimes, when Doc gets on a roll reading surveys, I think he's going to abruptly stop reading actual survey questions and break into one of his favorite musical numbers.

Doc always seems to be up for a game—any game. Provide him a lift and a few beverages, he's gonna hit that game of Wiffle in Timbuktu. Specifically, though, Doc loves baseball. He believes he would have had a shot at the Big Leagues if it weren't for a militant coach at his small liberal arts college who found fault with his then long hair—think Johnny Damon circa his Red Sox days. "You could start at Oberlin," the coach told Doc repeatedly. Relegated to the bench, Doc was arguably the best practice pinch runner his college has ever seen. After his freshman season, Doc retired from collegiate ball. Instead of the Show, Doc went on to coach high school (where he threw a mean batting practice), to pitch recreational softball—and to work a concession counter at Yankee Stadium. Unfortunately, working the counter keeps Doc in the corridor and he doesn't get to see much ball at all. I can visualize Doc at his post: he's pouring beers, keeping foam to an absolute minimum and picking up abandoned loose change off the counter as if it's lost treasure.

"Thank you," say the customers as Doc hands them their suds.

"No," Doc replies enthusiastically, pointing his finger. "Thank you!"

Though Doc doesn't get to see much of the actual game, just being in the stadium is rewarding.

At the ballpark, life is simpler. Most of the time, the harder I hawk, the more I make. When I enter the empty coliseum, I can practically feel the aura of Yankee Hall of Famer Lou Gehrig standing at home plate. "I consider myself the luckiest man on the face of this earth," Gehrig unforgettably told the crowd on the day of his final appearance. Being at the actual stadium, day in and day out, you do feel lucky. Batting practice—which I take in from the bleachers—is a soothing symphony, the periodic whack of the bats and the balls smacking leather. Walking the stairs gets the juices going, and barking out the names of the items is cathartic: when I bark, I do it with the enthusiasm of Aerosmith lead singer Steven Tyler. I see more baseball than I ever imagined. Just like the vendor locker room, the game grows on me. I follow the action a little, but not too closely. As the game plays out on the field, I play my own game, testing myself to see how much product I can move. I sell sodas with ill-fitting plastic covers that blow off at the merest hint of a slight breeze. I push the Green Monster, pitching it as a low-cal alternative to hot dogs. I work the pricey field-level seats, the land of the wealthy, where the Wall

Street crowd hits you with tips and stylish women flaunt their midriffs. On a few nights, I even reach the pinnacle of vending: I hawk beer, albeit not one of the popular brands. Still, it's an honor, especially for a rookie. Gradually, I evolve into somewhat of a salesman. I don't blindly shout. I *present* my product, climbing every stair of every aisle, to maximize my product's exposure to the widest possible audience. I frequently drop to my knees to avoid obstructing lines of vision and fully extend my body to hard-to-reach customers. Some vendors, specifically beer vendors, wear knee pads underneath their pants, to provide cushion. Beer vendors spend an inordinate time on their knees because pouring is a time-consuming process, and beer customers usually ask for more than one. Like many vendors, I walk at a brisk pace and consider myself somewhat of an athlete. I give accurate change. "You're doing something positive," one fan tells me.

———

Even when it's raining, I show up. The Yankees are making a run at the pennant, and I don't want to miss a single pitch. During the rain delay, I meet the Rookie, a Baltimore Orioles player, who had just been called up. In the slight drizzle, he's walking around left field near the seats. The Rookie is the sole individual on the field, and he has a starry-eyed look in his eyes, probably similar to the one I had during my vendor orientation. I'm in the first row with a few vendor colleagues, studying the manicured, wet grass as rain drops pelt the near-empty cathedral. It's peaceful. The Rookie and I are about the same age and somehow we start conversing. He looks up into the rows of empty seats and tries to envision what it will look like full. "It must be something," he says. As he surveys the empty seats, he wonders aloud if his ex will show. "She lives in the area," he says.

That day, the stands remained empty. It was a rain-out, and I didn't get paid. That's the thing about vending: it's commission plus tips. If you don't sell anything, you get nothing in return. Well, that's not completely true. The Rookie was the only player that I talked to the entire season.

We may work in the same building as the players, but we're definitely in different departments. Obviously, they're paid more, but they have exponentially more pressure. They have to earn that paycheck, day in, day out—show up, perform, and execute in front of a worldwide audience. If they don't, they're back on the street. We place professional athletes on a pedestal. It's deserved, for the most part. They possess superior physical skills and determination. It's no accident that they are where they are. Talent is only part of the equation. Hard work is the difference maker. Ultimately, the athletes are fragile like the rest of us. Time doesn't stop for them. They have a small window in which to peak. It could all end tomorrow with an injury. Then they're out of the circus, looking in like the rest of us. Then again, I'm not looking in. At least for now, I'm a part, albeit a small part, of the Show.

Not surprisingly, everything isn't charmed at the ballpark. A few vendors guard their assigned sections like personal fiefdoms. A few will take aggressive action if they believe that their section has been encroached on. During one afternoon game, a vendor came after me aggressively because he believed that I was an aisle into his assigned section. "Get out of here," he barked, pointing his finger. I thought he was an off-duty cop because of his authoritative tone. I retreated, not wanting to create a scene. I already knew that the guy was a jerk. Later, I learned that the guy was an accountant.

Another knuckle ball for vendors is dealing with belligerent fans, particularly inebriated ones. When a young fan, a punk, who's looking into his binoculars, barks, "Get the fuck out of my way, soda boy," I take exception. It's a weeknight game, kind of chilly, and sales are tepid. My wall isn't up, and I'm vulnerable. When I'm hawking, an attitude seems to give me an advantage. There are beer muscles, and then there are vendor muscles, not much difference between the two. After I've worked six innings holding the Monster, my vendor muscles are pulsing, and I'm ready for just about anything. As he peers through his binoculars, I stare at the wannabe tough guy like I'm staring down an opposing pitcher who just threw at my head. When he finally locates me through his lenses, Binocular Boy's expression turns to fear, perhaps even horror. When the inning ends, I go in—tray and all. In so many words, I tell him to watch who he's talking to, pointing my finger for emphasis. "OK," he offers apologetically.

The fans who sit in the six-dollar bleacher seats, which are actually benches, often act out, like European football hooligans. Nicknamed

Bleacher Creatures, they menace yuppies ("Everyone in a suit should be shot!") and playfully harass fans in the adjacent upper deck ("Jump!") and women ("Show us your tits!"). Belligerent behavior is the norm in the bleachers. Located in the outfield, they're basically a separate island compared to the rest of the stadium. Here, all the regulars know one another. Think *Cheers* with profanity and way, way more beer. There's the Queen of the Bleachers, a lean, tough-talking waitress who serves as the boss of the section. She controls practically everything, maintaining the mayhem, telling people when and how to cheer and whatnot. Stat Man, an unshaven, quiet man wearing a 1970s-style oversized headset, sits near the front making notations on his scorecard. In the back of the section, there's a designated person who bangs a cowbell to assist with the cheers. How do you get into this club of fanatics? Same way you get elite vendor status: you keep showing up.

Selling dogs requires more concentration than soda and other items. Each dog transaction is a quick (hopefully), methodical process. Right up front, I collect the cash and place it in my smock. If I allow that little matter to slip my mind, which is very possible considering there is an array of distractions, I'm picking up the tab. Then, I get down to the business of preparing the dog. Working as fast as I possibly can, I remove the bun from the plastic wrapping and place it in a napkin, making sure that the bun doesn't touch my bare hands. I spear the dog from the aluminum bin and place it in the bun. As far as condiments, I don't bother asking the customer their preferences. I just place some ketchup, mustard, and relish packets between the napkin and the dog. If they don't want the toppings, they'll toss the packets in my aluminum bin. Maybe they'll throw me a buck for my trouble. After being a vendor, I've become a much, much better tipper. It's funny how that works.

Selling dogs in the bleachers becomes my regular spot. I like the easy incline of the steps, and I appreciate the Creatures because they keep things interesting with their outrageous antics, and because they share a certain kinship with the vendors. They're the blue-collar fans, and we're the employees, who do the down-and-dirty work. They appreciate our work ethic and they save their vitriol for the opposing team—most of the time.

It's September, the Yankees are on the verge of making the playoffs, and I'm in my regular bleachers spot hawkin' dogs when I come across that intoxicated man who's doing everything in his power to make me feel uncomfortable. "I've got a hot dog hereyah!" he shouts as he points at his groin and thrusts his hips forward. "I've got a hot dog hereyah!" he repeats even louder, relentlessly baiting me. Everyone seems to be amused at the spectacle—everyone except me. I'm embarrassed. With all the excitement, my vendor muscles are in mid-game form, and I want to confront him verbally like I did with the binoculars punk. I'm ready for a showdown. Call it Drunk Man versus Wienie Man. . . . But something stops me, and I don't engage. Instead, I turn my back, walk in the opposite direction, and carry on. Soon enough, the situation dissipates. This is how you tame a heckler. Whether you're a player or a vendor, just ignore a heckler. It'll do the trick. I promise.

Right before the playoffs, my long-lost editor, Felix, whom I haven't heard from all season, calls. It's not a complete surprise that we haven't spoken. My article isn't supposed to run for a while, and the Mag is swamped with its launch. When we finally connect, Felix has no time for pleasantries. "Where's your copy?" he snaps impatiently.

"I'm still working at the stadium."

"You're *where*!?" he asks incredulously.

"I'm at the stadium," I reply calmly. "I'm working."

In my defense, he hasn't given me much guidance, no parameters, no deadline. I just took the ball and ran with it. Things were going well. Why quit?

"You're the George Costanza of journalism!" Felix laughs. He's not laughing with me. I don't mention that I've convinced my friend, Doc, to enlist in stadium work. Felix would probably snort back: *What! Are your parents working there, too? How about your cousins?*

"Just keep track of your expenses," Felix finally says, exasperated. Felix is pretty cool about expenses. He picked up the tab for all post-game pretzels.

During the playoffs, tensions mount as the Yankees show signs of faltering. Fans and vendors alike are ultra-fragile. With the season's end imminent, I'm brooding over my next move, and so is Hustle, who's down. He's considering going back to school or becoming a cop, of all things, as he's not exactly a rules and regulations guy. "I'm still young," he tells me. "I need another job."

Doc is experiencing bouts of anxiety as well. "I could work at a gym!" he shouts at me during one of our memorable back-and-forths.

Morale hits a low when the rookie vendor locker room is burglarized. "Only n—s steal behind your back," yells a furious vendor. Fortunately, I never stored anything of value in that sweltering, gloomy box that had become somewhat of second home. When I mention the episode to one of my reporter colleagues, it reminds me of the insular, very white newspaper world that I'm on the fringes of. He's taken aback and offended by the liberal use of the N word, something that I've become accustomed to in the vending world. When I describe Charlie Hustle's appearance, he's genuinely surprised.

"Charlie Hustle's black?" he asks.

"Very, extremely, dark chocolate," I want to respond. Instead, I just keep my mouth shut. At this point, I haven't done enough to earn sarcasm.

Fortunately, the Yankees make it to the World Series. I'm psyched. I'm not ready for the season to end. Unfortunately, Game One is a washout, literally. Doc is on full alert, constantly listening to sports radio and keeping a vigilant eye on the weather reports. Every few hours we touch base and he delivers his forecast. "It looks as though it's heading north," Doc says as he examines the radar on his television. "We'll be playing ball soon." Doc—he's a good egg. I'll trust him with the ball in the late innings of a tight game of our coed, slow-pitch softball league. However, I'm still out on his meteorology skills.

"You sure?" I inquire skeptically.

"Yeah I'm sure," Doc replies. "But let me check, just to be *completely* sure." Doc watches the radar and goes silent.

"What's wrong?" I ask.

He groans. I can practically see Doc shake his head.

"It doesn't look good. *We* might not play for *days*."

Then, Doc pauses.

"*Days, Jon!*"

After days and days of similar exchanges, the rain ceases and the Fall Classic commences. Before the games against the Atlanta Braves begin, my fellow vendors and I sit in the stands and soak it all in. Everything feels different, even the air. It's hardball in October. "This is World Series batting practice," Baltimore announces excitedly before Game One, as hordes of media types amble by, ignoring him just as his fellow vendors do. Baltimore taunts the incoming crowd with tomahawk chops. He's embarrassing but no one can control him, except maybe the Boss, who is nowhere to be seen. Fortunately, just about everyone ignores Baltimore, who claims that he's flying down to Atlanta to work those games as well. Meanwhile, Doc has moved up the counter worker ladder and has been upgraded to a glamour spot, a personal stand replete with an umbrella, right behind home plate, where fans leave the action and wait inning after inning after inning to get concessions, something that Doc can't quite fathom. At Doc's new assignment, the tips are decent and the clientele is high-end. One night, unexpectedly, Doc comes face-to-face with an old pal, Yankees outfielder Paul O'Neill's older brother, Mike, whom Doc knew during his formative years when he had his long hair. As a reward for making the Series, the Boss had flown in the players' family members. When Mike spotted Doc at his stand in his Good Humor getup, his facial expression must have been priceless. That night, they got reacquainted, perhaps to the chagrin of the customers waiting in Doc's line. When inspired, Doc can be quite the conversationalist.

After the Yankees get slaughtered in the first two games, everyone's understandably somber. Concessions sales die.

No one can eat *a thing*.

With the series going to Atlanta for the next three games, vendors bid their farewell.

Then, something magical happens. The Yankees snare the next three games in Atlanta to bring the series back to New York for the clincher—hopefully. Game Six completely grips the city. It has been eighteen years. As usual, Doc checks in at the stadium a few hours before first pitch as he's supposed to, but he *doesn't* report to his assigned glamour position. Tonight's special, and Doc is watching the game—finally. He deserves it. Besides stealing a glance here and there at the action on field, he's been stuck in the corridor, resigned to pouring beer, pocketing loose change, and listening to the crowd. Since there are absolutely no seats available, Doc watches the game from the entrances of the different sections, moving every few innings, so he won't be detected by security.

Later, Doc would make it seem like he was on some kind of covert CIA mission. With his flair for the dramatic, I can just imagine Doc telling his grandchildren about it decades later: *Security was everywhere . . . but I found an opening, got away, and saw Game Six!* In retrospect, no one was probably watching Doc too closely. Everyone was too absorbed by the epic event at hand. At the entrance, Yankees gatekeepers were taking $20 bribes from fans and allowing them to sneak in. Back then, real tickets were the norm. It was pre-9/11 and you didn't have to be frisked at the door. Game Six, 1996: it turned out to be one of New York's last great parties before the city—and the world—changed.

After five innings, the crowd's energy intensifies and hot dog sales stop. Sales hadn't been that great to begin with during the post-season, unless you were Doc or one of the elite veteran vendors who got to sell special programs, which were going for something like $25 a pop. I heard that there was one very fortunate souvenir vendor who earned $8,000 selling Yankee paraphernalia during Game Six alone. Call him the Eight Thousand Dollar Man. In the post-season, the actual game on the field takes center stage. As far as the dogs, well, fans have the rest of their lives for that. In my personal game, I'm hustling hard to get whatever sales I can muster. I want to play *my* game 'til the last possible out. As usual, I see little of Game Six. I don't really need to. I can feel it. When I walk up the steps, I can't help but notice that *all* eyes are focused intently on the field.

Heading into the sixth, the Yankees are leading and everyone's standing. It's so close to being over. Of course, I don't want it to be. My every move becomes monumental. In a nod to Doc, I dramatically remove my price badge and hand it to a woman who says that she's an MTV VJ. I go to the Pit, pay up, and check out. I don't go to the locker room. Instead, I head to the field-level seats, right behind third base, where the Man, the editor in chief of the Mag—not Felix—is sitting. This is a first. The ballpark has been my oasis, and I've successfully kept my two worlds separate. At the stadium, I haven't hung out with any non-ballpark co-workers, civilians—until now. It's cool to hang out with the Man. But it's also somewhat awkward. There's a disconnect. Understandably, the Man wants to enjoy the final outs like everyone else. I, on the other hand, want to talk vendor minutiae. For the past few months, vending has been my game, my diversion, my obsession. With the Man, to whom I handed my uniform as a souvenir, I manage to restrain myself. I attempt to focus on the game and be a civilian, a fan. When the Yankees win, everyone rejoices 1999 style even though it's 1996. We belt out "New York, New York" and "We Are the Champions" as Wade Boggs rides a policeman's horse around the field. Look up "glorious moment" in the dictionary. This is it!

―――――

When I wake up the next morning, I'm hung over, not from anything I imbibed or inhaled with Doc but from all the emotion and the realization that my vendor journey has come to an end. Now, though, I've got to move on, but to what? I have no prospects. I check the calendar: only five months 'til Opening Day. I miss vending. I pine for all its aspects, everything from the physicality to the vendor characters, even Baltimore. I still talk to Doc, of course, but our conversations lack the urgency that's inherent with an eighteen-year drought. Now, *we've* won a championship, so we're understandably more mellow.

I want *my* game back.

Days later, I head down to Madison Square Garden and land a job. No problem. The Garden even pays health benefits. I could be doing this for a while. When the Man, the editor in chief at the Mag, somehow finds out that I'm back in the vending game, I hear that he's pleasantly amused, comparing me to Marlon Brando's character in *Apocalypse Now*, who goes out on assignment and winds up becoming completely consumed. At the Garden, I sell popcorn, a low-level item, to Knicks and Rangers fans. It's not the same as the ballpark. Sadly, the folks in the Garden's cheap seats don't want popcorn, not one kernel. It's not just the item that's bothering me. Relative to Yankee Stadium, the Garden is small, and I feel like I'm constantly walking in circles. If there's a heckler who's bothering me, I can't keep my distance. Besides that, everything's inside and the place has the feel of a corporate vacuum. It's basically an after-work venue where people dress to impress. I've got nothing better on the horizon, so I attempt to stick it out for as long as possible, at least through the holiday season. I figure I'll make a few bucks, and I do mean a few. Before Christmas, at the Garden's adjacent theater, I dress up like a nineteenth-century dandy to push product, mostly sweets, including cookies and cotton candy, during the holiday run of *A Christmas Carol*. It's a big seller with my new clientele, mostly rambunctious kids on school trips. I'm keeping busy, working four shows a day, but I'm ready to move on. Before New Year's, I hand in my Dickens garb for good.

———

Just weeks after I waved the white flag, Brownie, a former editor from the paper, invites me to the Garden for a Knicks game.

Brownie had given me one of my first assignments: covering a treadmill marathon. At the time, I was delivering newspapers at all hours with an ex-con, who, well, wanted me to disappear. Frankly, I was too exhausted to be intimidated. I was ragged and probably didn't smell like petunias. "You look like you fell out of a Dumpster," Brownie would often tell me in his faint Southern drawl when I'd stagger into his office. Thankfully, Brownie threw me the treadmill marathon assignment, which I was ecstatic to get. So on a Saturday, I attended the marathon, ready to report. Not surprisingly, the treadmill marathon was a snore. Within an hour, I put down my notebook and pen and mounted one of the treadmills, to the bemusement of the small crowd, which was basically the treadmill marathon public relations team. "He's actually going to run!" I overheard Publicist A tell Publicist B. Indeed, I ran, seven-plus miles, before I picked up my pad and resumed taking notes.

After we both departed the paper, Brownie and I remained in touch. We'd often meet for heated one-on-one basketball battles. When he invited me to the Garden, I wanted no part of it. Nothing against Brownie, I just didn't feel like returning to my former workplace. It made me understand why waiters don't care much for eating in their own dining establishments. I think the Knicks were playing the Celtics, or maybe it was the Pistons—I really didn't care. From our seats behind the basket, I watched the game I *truly* knew: I was studying my former colleagues and their work habits. At one point, a vendor stopped in front of my section. Neither I, nor anyone in my section, had signaled for him. He walked up the flight of stairs, put down his tray of soda, and embraced me. It was nice to be reunited with one of my brethren. Meanwhile, I felt the eyes of my section neighbors. I imagine that most people with overpriced Knick tickets don't know vendors. If I could hawk their facial expressions. . . . As for Brownie, he was very impressed.

———

A few years after that wonderful, unforgettable 1996 season, Doc finally got his due: he was finally called up to the Show. He had waited long enough. Years after his college career as a practice runner, when he was in his thirties, Doc hadn't given up on making it to the Big Leagues. He even answered an open call in *The Sporting News* looking for prospects, and he flew down to Florida on his own dime. Playing against nineteen- and twenty-year olds, Doc opened the eyes of a few scouts. Unfortunately, nothing came to fruition. Finally, after he had won over legions of Yankees fans with his affable counter manner, Doc got the nod. Mike, Paul O'Neill's older brother, invited him to a World Series game. And when the Yankees clinched yet another world championship, Doc was invited down to the inner sanctum, the Yankees locker room, where the Yankees were celebrating. In a small training room, a crevice of the stadium, Doc celebrated with Joe Torre, Joe Girardi, Paul O'Neill, and Tino Martinez, among others. It's fair to say that the Yankees didn't have a clue that they were talking to a former all-star Yankee Stadium concessionaire. Torre told Doc that he was certain that Roger Clemens would deliver, how Roger wanted to ensure his legacy by winning a ring. Within moments, Doc and the first baseman had a repartee and were on a first-name basis, at least on Doc's end. "Tino was talking about how he was looking forward to going home to Tampa to work out," Doc told me. "For a guy like me, it was pretty cool."

3

School of Hard Knocks

I became a professional wrestling student completely by accident. While researching boxing at the legendary Gleason's Gym, I found myself intrigued with the in-house pretenders, students of the Unpredictable School, the professional wrestling school at Gleason's that serves as a pipeline for professional wrestling's minor leagues. Amid the scores of boxers, a few wrestlers were practicing, playfully tossing themselves around the ring. It didn't look too strenuous.

Days later, I got in touch with the Man and informed him that I was ready to matriculate at a professional wrestling school. When I mentioned that the school charged a hefty fee, I figured that he'd balk, but the Mag began footing my bill, unbeknown to the school. (For a lifetime membership to his Unpredictable School, Johnny Rodz, a former pro, was charging students up to three thousand dollars, not including Gleason's forty-five-dollar monthly gym fee.) Rodz took all comers, no experience required.

Early on, Rodz proclaimed that I had what it takes to make it in the business. Maybe he was right. How hard could it be? Pro wrestling is an act, and I'd had some theater training. I even played a wrestler in my college's production of *As You Like It*. Plus, I had wrestled in high school for one miserable year. I had never gotten into it, just going through the motions.

I was trying to impress the opposite sex. Unfortunately, a sense of humor will only go so far. Believe me.

I was a legit wrestler who was pretending.

> I am still playing make-believe. One time, I pretended to be a
> reporter. A friend in public relations—the genius behind the

treadmill marathon—asked me to attend a luncheon with the handlers of an up-and-coming heavyweight boxer. I had no interest. I didn't think that I could drum up any interest in the fighter, a man they were hyping as the next great white hope. However, my friend desperately needed bodies, *any body*, to make it appear as if there was interest. And he wanted to make it appear as if he was doing his job. After several desperate calls, I reluctantly agreed. At the luncheon, a family-style Italian feast of epic proportions, the handlers believed that they were holding court with members of the media elite. The reality: besides myself, they were dining with cronies from my PR friend's high school class. They were all regular guys, mostly salesmen. For the feast, though, they were all posing as reporters. Between courses, I nodded politely as the salesmen hit the boxer's entourage with questions.

Early on in my Unpredictable School education, I learned that there are few, if any, overnight successes in big-time professional wrestling. For starters, the World Wrestling Federation (WWF) wouldn't even consider wannabe mat men without three to five years of pro wrestling experience. The other major wrestling organization at the time, World Championship Wrestling (WCW), required a three-day tryout just for the privilege of paying three thousand dollars for their six-month course.

During class, Rodz is full of encouragement. "You already look like a wrestler," exclaims the man who counts pros like Tazz, Damian Demento, and Tommy Dreamer among his successful disciples. Rodz's office at Gleason's is a shrine to the sport, covered with photos of legendary mat men, including David Schultz, the wrestler who went after television reporter John Stossel.

Rodz, a member of the WWF's Hall of Fame, had tasted the big time, rising to prominence in the late 1970s while donning an Arabian kaffiyeh and performing across the country. The highlight of his career came at Los Angeles's Olympic Auditorium in 1976, when, fighting under the name of Java Ruuk, he outlasted superstars André the Giant and Ric Flair in a twenty-two-wrestler Battle Royale. The glory was short-lived, however, and for the better portion of his career Rodz was a "jobber," a regular loser on Saturday morning television, whose role was to build the headliner resumes. Now, his job was to build up wannabe pretenders like myself.

"You can do it, if you put the time in," Rodz tells me one day after class. "Anyone can." However, my fellow students aren't so sure. Amid these mat men, I feel small. My fellow classmates recommend that I bulk up. During my high school wrestling stint, I trained in boiler rooms and dieted on water and lettuce doused in vinegar trying to make weight. In professional wrestling, the performers want to get huge, larger than life.

The Unpredictable School is aptly named. When you show up for class, you never quite know what to expect. At the School, the wrestlers work out together, with the veterans teaching the younger guys. My first mentor is Bruno, a crusty marshmallow of a man. Bruno boasts that he has wrestled "everywhere." I immediately envision him as a demigod in some far-off land. I press him on where he has performed. "Brooklyn and Queens," he grunts.

Lesson one has Bruno showing me how to move around the ring. As we lock up in an awkward waltz, he slaps my arm. "Relax!" he barks. "You're tense." Between the ropes, Bruno teaches me the tricks of the trade. He insists that we face each other at all times, so that we're prepared for the other person's upcoming move. He says we should remain flexible so that we can manipulate one another with minimal resistance. I'm ordered to keep my elbows down as a matter of etiquette. Exposing an elbow to a fellow wrestler in the ring is the equivalent of taking a swing at him with a police officer's nightstick. As I hesitatingly follow Bruno's massive lead, he embraces me, so his cheek is next to my ear, so that we can communicate if necessary.

As the early weeks of training progress, I find I'm having difficulty mastering the most essential part of the game—the art of falling. Falling *is* professional wrestling—the louder the better. Once a wrestler knows how to fall properly, he (or she) can be tossed around the ring by any opponent. At that point, you're more than halfway to making a living. As part of my basic training, I'm required to fall straight back, and crash onto the mat, landing just below my shoulder blades. This is punctuated by swatting the mat with both open palms, which accentuates the crash even more and adds to the illusion of a near-fatal impact. It's easier said than done.

There's also an element of danger to falling: a wrestler must keep his head glued to his neck and not allow it to slam into the mat. This is essential to avoid losing consciousness and perhaps worse. Done correctly, the thunderous collision of a fall can be heard above the rat-a-tat-tat of the aspiring boxers pounding Gleason's speed bags. Done incorrectly, you very well could be on your way to intensive care. I proceed to fall, albeit somewhat awkwardly, for several weeks. Often, several of my fellow wrestlers shake their heads disapprovingly. I stay out of the emergency room, but I suffer countless headaches and survive on a steady diet of Advil. Fellow wrestlers promise that I'll become acclimated and that the headaches will disappear with time. Desperate, I try everything to conquer my fear of falling. At one point, I even resort to a relaxation technique that I learned from one of my acting teachers, where I stand still and shake my hands vigorously. My college director, who coincidentally was the one to cast me as the wrestler Chuck the Chewer in *As You Like It*, would have certainly approved . . . or maybe he would've been appalled like Spanish Angel, a strapping up-and-comer who wears a black leather mask during matches. When he observes me shaking my body vigorously, like I'm having some sort of seizure attack, Spanish Angel just rolls his eyes.

———

Finally, after months of crashing into the ring, I make my debut in a matinee showcase at Gleason's. Fifty or so customers have come to see some of Rodz's disciples grapple. As a sideshow, the school's rookies have been instructed to demonstrate some killer falls. When my number comes up, I tell myself to relax, to fall within myself. Unfortunately, the rest is blurry. As I go through my requisite, unspectacular tumbles, I fear that I'm losing both the crowd and my composure. Sadly, I'm not showing them anything they haven't seen before. Almost tragically, I'm not showing them anything that they *want* to see. I feel like a late-night stand-up comic whose lame punch lines are lost to the audience's inebriated state. The spectators want something big. I want to bring it and give 'em their money's worth. (Yes, they are actually paying for this.)

I try to fall harder than I've ever fallen, but my landing is a relative muffle. Worse, forgetting everything I've learned, I forget my form and my head bounces off the mat. Dazed, I struggle to get up and once again hurl myself wildly. After I fall, I'm disoriented. The audience is disinterested. I'm drowsy, starting to lose consciousness, but I manage to stagger up and bounce off the ropes before once again falling onto the mat, quietly. No one cares. When I step out of the ring, the crowd is silent.

Embarrassed, I strongly consider hanging up my tights—that is if I had tights. Instead, I stick it out, working out as much as I can with Unpredictable's unusual breed of characters, an array of quirky true believers and slightly fanatical wannabes. One young wrestler, who was steered toward the school by his high school guidance counselor, went off to follow the Ultimate Warrior, an immensely popular character. "He's fuckin' crazy," says Rodz.

Others seem to be completely sane and completely committed to the dream that has refused to die ever since they watched wrestling as youngsters. Kid USA, for one, seems to have the goods. He has long blond hair and an athletic physique, and he can really rassle. He even has a compelling gimmick, a proven formula that Hulk Hogan used to transform himself into a household name. Announced at matches as being from Any Town, USA, the Kid proudly strides toward the ring, his finger pointing upward, his other hand waving Old Glory as James Brown's "Living in America" blares. Accompanied by a statuesque female (apparently his real-life girlfriend), he even sells "red, white, and blue" paraphernalia at matches. "He believes it's real," a fellow wrestler whispers to me. Therein lies the secret of his success.

Then there's the Musketeer. A polished suburbanite, the Musketeer speaks in complete sentences, has a flat stomach, and stretches for fifteen minutes before practicing, for which he is sometimes teased by the other wrestlers. One of the school's most diligent workers, he drives an hour and a half each way to practice. "One day I'll be on television," he tells me, a wistful took in his eyes.

Most intriguing of all is a wrestler with seemingly world-class moves. Called simply the Sheik, he bears a striking resemblance to the Iron Sheik, the wrestler who came to prominence in the 1980s as Sgt. Slaughter's nemesis. Inside the ropes, the Sheik is a master. No one at Unpredictable feigns a better punch than the Sheik. He flinches and shakes as sweat rolls off his bald head. "What the hell ya got?" he taunts opponents in a heavy accent more Bronx than Baghdad. With the Sheik, nothing seems fake. At one point, he tells me about the backaches he incurred mixing it up with legend Tony Atlas. "I'm too old for this shit," he sighs. Rodz tells me that the Sheik doesn't wrestle much anymore. He works as an armed security guard and comes to work out at his leisure. After months of working out at Gleason's, I'm quite certain that the Sheik is *not* the actual Iron Sheik—but he sure looks like him. So while I never worked out with the wrestling legend, I can always say that I worked out with a legend lookalike.

As the months wear on, I feel as though I'm not progressing. The reality is that I'm not very good at wrestling. Invariably, I'm told that I'm falling the wrong way or not tumbling correctly by, well, just about the entire Unpredictable student body. Sadly, I don't have the same passion or talent that my classmates have. Eventually, I become a wrestling school dropout. Rodz is persistent, though, calling me, attempting to lure me back. Frustrated, I tell him that I possess no wrestling talent and that I have no shot at being the next Hulk Hogan, or something to that effect. "You gotta give yourself a chance," Rodz pleads. "I've seen you skate—whatever the heck you do—and you're great!" Rodz adds that my "natural look" would prove popular with promoters. I want to believe Rodz, who seems to sincerely care about his wrestlers, spending hours with them in his office conversing about "the business." Ultimately, Rodz's pep talk does the trick, and I head back to Gleason's and resolve to myself to suck up the pain. With renewed vigor, I somersault across the mat and bounce off the metal ropes. I learn how to "punch" fellow wrestlers by hitting them with an upward slap and in return get slapped, repeatedly, which, as usual, doesn't feel fake. I learn how to clothesline a wrestler by delivering a semi-erect stiff arm to the chest.

Somewhere along the way, I'm deemed ready to engage in the pièce de résistance of wrestling maneuvers: the body slam. Draped over a man's broad shoulders, about to be body slammed, I desperately want to be put down. Before I can back out, my fellow wrestler hoists me in the air.

As I begin my descent toward the mat, I shut my eyes and brace myself for impact. When I finally land, my eyes remain completely shut—and I don't get up. "Slam the mat!" one of my colleagues hollers at me, pounding his hand onto the canvas for emphasis. Fortunately, I'm very much alive to take the very public scolding. I learn this repeatedly: first and foremost, pro wrestling is painful. Some fans question how pro wrestlers can take steroids. After actually experiencing their work, I wonder how can they not.

The Unpredictable student body makes it clear that what happens inside the ring is only half the game. The gimmick is equally important. No ambiguity required. It's strictly black-and-white: you're either a good guy (a baby face à la Kid USA) or a bad guy (a heel like the real Iron Sheik). Subtlety is not wanted. For many, this is wrestling's allure. For kids, the comic book good-versus-evil themes are easy to understand. Adults like it for the same reason.

When the time is right, Rodz takes his students aside and assigns each a persona. It's a wrestler's rite of passage. At one point, the towering bald teacher with the NFL player's build becomes Mr. Clean. The chubby ex-high school football player starts to wear a Stetson and is transformed into the Outlaw. The long haired construction worker emerges as that role model for flag-waving boy scouts—Kid USA.

Rodz never officially assigns me a gimmick. Nevertheless, I come up with my own: Johnny Love, a fun-loving, Venice Beach party guy who likes to dance on blades. For my entrance, I envision bungee jumping on my blades from the top of the arena, before performing a series of pirouettes around the ring. After showing off my moves, I chat up the audience, handing out samples from my long blond wig. When I tell Rodz a condensed version of my grand plan, he just smiles politely. I can't blame Rodz for his lack of enthusiasm. In retrospect, I seriously regret the concept.

I'm not a wrestler. I'm the opening act for ABBA.

For my first Unpredictable School field trip, we hit a high school gym in Nowheresville, New Jersey—otherwise known as Lacey Township. I'm attending an actual match, where some of Unpredictable's higher-caliber students will be performing on the same card as wrestling legends.

When we arrive at the gym, I immediately start devising a plan to get into the evening's final match, the Battle Royale, which pits a dozen or so wrestlers against one another. It seems like an unlikely reach, as I'm still a novice between the ropes.

As the kids and parents enter, two legends—Greg "The Hammer" Valentine, and King Kong Bundy—sit stone-faced, charging kids a few bucks for autographed photos. As for customers, it's slim pickings: the gym is only a quarter full to see the aforementioned wrestlers, as well as fellow legends Tony Atlas and Jimmy "Superfly" Snuka. As I take a seat in the bleachers, I'm anxious to see how the evening plays out. I'm particularly curious to see how my colleagues will do. I'm rooting for them—for real.

In the night's opening match, the Musketeer is wrestling in one of his first shows. To reach this point, the Musketeer has undergone at least a year of rigorous training that has transformed him into an acrobat and illusionist, capable of launching off the top turnbuckle and drop-kicking a man's chest while making it appear he's connecting with his esophagus. Inevitably, since he's the good guy, the Musketeer wins. In professional wrestling, the virtuous only lose when the bad guy happens to be a Big-Name Bad Guy, in which case the promoters allow him to win via various dirty tricks. As the Musketeer leaves the ring, cheering kids rush over to touch him, and he departs confident but relieved, reminiscent of an actor who's not completely certain of his lines but who manages to pull off a compelling performance nevertheless.

For all his energy tonight, the Musketeer pockets a few dollars, if anything. At this point, he just wants experience. The marquee names aren't raking in much more, though. In professional wrestling, at least at this level, no one's making much. (After the matches are done for the evening, the promoters and some of the wrestlers will engage in a very real argument over cash.)

Toward the end of the night, the former superstars grapple, but the few hundred in attendance have had enough, and the old-timers' performances have all the sizzle of an exhausted vaudeville routine. I can't fault the audience. They're mostly kids, and it's late on a school night.

Ultimately, I don't make the Battle Royale cut. I remain in the bleachers, headache free, taking in the illusion of controlled mayhem. As two wrestlers tangle, a kid next to me comments: "It doesn't look real."

During the match, I decide to end my wrestling journey. On the ride back with the other wrestlers, I fall asleep in the car, relieved that I don't have to pretend anymore.

4

Smells Like Team Spirit

I never wanted to be a mascot.

I never imitated the Phillie Phanatic's tongue release, and not once did I mimic the gait of the San Diego Chicken. However, in retrospect, I showed mascot tendencies all along. After a demoralizing high school soccer defeat, I started to disrobe in public as a motivational tactic. My efforts produced some inspiration, few victories, and the attention of the cheerleading squad, who wanted to tap into my enthusiasm and offered me a spot on their roster. Unfortunately for them, I was off to college.

There, our school mascot, Charlie Catamount, was generally ignored, a tragic fate for any costumed cheerleader. All mascots long to be either embraced or reviled, but at the very least acknowledged. Yet despite the fact that I never auditioned for the thankless position, one of my classmates, Newmark, spread a false rumor that I was suiting up as Charlie. Unfortunately, the rumor seemed plausible, as I was very supportive of the men's basketball team. Years later, that rumor lives on and occasionally at gatherings when former classmates approach, they ask, "What was it like to be Charlie Catamount?"

I ignored any latent mascot tendencies—that is, until I heard about a mascot audition for the CityHawks, New York's new arena league football team. I figured I had a shot at getting the gig. Plus, mascot work looked like a cakewalk compared to the brutal world of professional wrestling.

In preparation for the audition, I did some homework. I learned that it's no easy proposition to become the next San Diego Chicken, especially in New York, where there are a wealth of professional sports teams but a dearth of mascot opportunities. Yes, the Mets send out the bulbous, baseball-headed Mr. Met, but after that, there's not so much. When the CityHawks held a tryout for its mascot, Sid T. Hawk, I knew it was a rare opportunity. Promptly, I mentioned it to one of my editors, Joel, who assigned me to chronicle my audition.

———

Coincidentally, Joel had also assigned me to write about the Rangers unofficial mascot Dancing Larry, a diehard Rangers fan who danced in between periods to the delight of the Madison Square Garden rowdies. For that, I returned to the Garden's cheap seats, where mere months ago I was relentlessly heckled and booed when I attempted to hawk popcorn. (No surprise, these rowdies only wanted one thing: beer.) Over the course of the game, I interviewed Dancing Larry. Before he started dancing at Rangers games, Dancing Larry was Larry Goodman, just another Jersey guy who was working at a chain music store. Larry wanted more than the retail life had to offer. He just didn't know what. At one point, Larry tried acting classes. When Dancing George, another dancing Rangers fan, missed a few games, Larry saw his opportunity and promptly got up and started shaking it. Ever since, Larry hasn't stopped dancing.

Interviewing Dancing Larry and his friends was only the first portion of my work for the evening. Unfortunately, Joel wanted something else. He needed a quote, just one quote, from Rangers defenseman/enforcer Jeff Beukeboom for an unrelated piece. Specifically, Joel wanted me to get a quote from Beukeboom in response to Rangers goalie Mike Richter's remark that Beukeboom had "a huge ass." Without thinking, I agreed to wrangle a quote from Beukeboom. As I wandered down to the Rangers locker room, I was berating myself for agreeing to do it. It wasn't my article, and I wasn't getting compensated for the extra work, which just might get me punched out. Also, it just wasn't my style. I interview the goofy guy dancing in the stands. I don't provoke players, particularly ones that are 6-foot-5 and serve as their team's enforcer. (Beukeboom is second on the Rangers all-time list for penalty minutes logged.) But I didn't want to wimp out.

With my press pass draped around my neck, I had no trouble getting back to the changing area. Behind the scenes, it was nothing like I imagined: there was chaos, equipment everywhere, guys on walkie-talkies. With no uniforms and last names on their jerseys, I couldn't tell any of the players apart. In street clothes, these hockey guys looked like everyone else. (In fact, a year or so earlier, at a Rangers fundraiser that I was covering, one fan confused me for Rangers player Sergei Nemchinov.) For a few minutes, I walked around the post-game confusion, hoping that Beukeboom had left the building. Meanwhile, I worked on my alibi for Joel. *I tried. I really did. But the man dressed within minutes and was gone. VANISHED!* I asked around and someone pointed him out, unfortunately. You couldn't miss him. He was by far the largest man in the locker room area. At a doorway, I apprehensively introduced myself. He looked down at me, all ears. I guess I looked official enough with my press pass, which did not specify that I was just there to interview the dancing, goofy guy—not players. There was no time for bunnies, the warm-up questions.

"I just have one question."

"Sure," he said. Fortunately, he seemed in a non-violent mood. Maybe he wouldn't punch me in the face.

"I'm sure this was said in jest," I muttered quickly, holding out my recorder as he waited. "Richter . . . ," I sputtered. "Richter says you have a huge ass," I somehow managed to finally get out. "Care to comment?"

For a moment, he said nothing.

"Is that so?" Beukeboom finally said.

I braced myself.

Fortunately, Beukeboom broke into a broad smile. He wasn't gonna ram my head through the wall after all. He was amused. In fact, he acted like a complete gentleman and delivered a very polite, brief, generic response, which Joel's publication never used. I thanked Beukeboom profusely and left the Garden, pleased that I had interviewed Dancing Larry and ecstatic that Beukeboom hadn't beat the shit out of me.

After the episode, I envisioned an interview with a potential editor, who's looking over my resume:

> EDITOR: So it says here that you've interviewed professional athletes.
> ME: Well, ah, it was actually only one athlete, but . . .
> EDITOR: Who?

ME: Beukeboom . . . Jeff Beukeboom.
EDITOR: Great, where did it run?
ME: Well, it didn't.
EDITOR: It was killed?
ME: Yes, kind of . . . It's a long story.
EDITOR: Well, what was your angle?
ME: It just didn't work out.
EDITOR: Well, what did you ask him?
ME: I just asked him one question.
EDITOR: *What* was the question?
ME: I don't know.
EDITOR: You don't know!
ME: I know the question. I mean . . . I don't know if I should say.
EDITOR: Just say it. I'm a busy editor. You're wasting—
ME: OK, this was the question: Richter says you have a huge ass. Care to comment?

Cut to awkward silence.

———

In comparison, I figure that the Sid T. Hawk audition would be relatively easy sailing. Shortly after I arrive at the tryout, though, I learn that my competition is formidable. I'm pitted against two industry veterans: a former Easter Bunny and a guy who used to dress up as a zombie and scare hay riders in a cemetery. I'm a bit timid at first. Eventually, I pull out my secret weapon: my in-line skates. Anyone can cheer and jump and shout. I can do it on blades!

My competitors and I dance and clown our hearts out in front of a gaggle of television crews filming the spectacle, not to mention a throng of auditioning cheerleaders. A colleague, who's covering the story for the *New York Post*, just shakes his head in disbelief as I shriek, splay my wings, and even perform a set of push-ups, clapping my hands between repetitions. Again, I'm doing this all on blades.

I haven't won much in my life. Yes, there was the perfect attendance award in grade school and I was the most improved tennis player in my age group at summer camp. After that, well, I'm still thinking . . . Ultimately, I smoke the former Easter Bunny and the Zombie and win that mascot competition. I'm not alone in my thinking. A female reporter goes so far as to say this: "If you don't get the job, it will be a crime against humanity." Following the audition, I'm bombarded by questions from reporters—and I just roll with it.

"Why are you doing this?"

"Sid T. Hawk is my destiny. There's nothing else!" I answer. Next question!

"How do you feel about your performance?"

"I left it all out on the floor!"

"Why do you want the job?" asks local television reporter Curt Menefee, whom I happen to recognize.

"To be as close as possible to the cheerleaders!"

That evening, the audition goes viral over the local news, and the following day, long-lost friends surface to congratulate me on my ridiculous performance. "I always thought you were underappreciated as Charlie Catamount," cracks Newmark.

Joel is satisfied. However, I want more. I actually want the gig! I could do it. Sadly, the CityHawks brass weren't as impressed as that female reporter, and they didn't make me an offer. Actually, they didn't even give me a courtesy call. Later, I learned that the contest was a sham, a cheap, shameless media publicity ploy. They never intended to hire anyone from the tryout. Ironically, my participation in the tryout seemed to disqualify me from actually getting the position. Ultimately, I was a mascot wannabe who knew too much.

———

Not long after this, I come across Mascot Mania, a mascot school located in Nashville, and I contact the school's teacher, Dean Schoenewald, who has suited up for at least eighteen teams in a wide variety of sports leagues, ranging from the North American Soccer League (NASL) to the United States Football League (USFL), during his lengthy career. Schoenewald promises that he'll not only teach me the mascot trade but also direct me toward a mascot job. He adds that the Mets are looking to fill the Mr. Met character. After hearing Schoenewald's spiel, I make plans to hit Nashville and see where it goes.

Days later, I'm on a Greyhound headed south, on my own dime. I hadn't even bothered to mention it to the Mag. I basically assigned the adventure to myself. Over the course of the twenty-one-hour ride, my mind does cartwheels as I imagine meeting my mascot brethren, my partners in mime. Perhaps we'd trade war stories of unfulfilled athletic dreams. In vain, I attempt to stop my relentless daydreaming and catch some shut-eye.

When I finally arrive, I'm disappointed to learn that no other students had enrolled in the three-day session. Perhaps the school's $800 fee had kept them away. To make matters worse, I haven't gotten much sleep during the crowded ride. Fortunately, I don't have to do much work right off the bat. Schoenewald immediately whisks me off to a lecture he's giving before a business class at Vanderbilt University, where he has spoken three times previously. At Vanderbilt, the man who has personally tutored such mascot luminaries as the Chicago Bulls' Da Bull commences his speech by proclaiming himself to be one of the "craziest men in sports." For the next hour, the class is rapt as Schoenewald enthusiastically lauds his trade. His message to the students is loud and clear: the mascot industry is wide open and growing. *Mascots are expanding beyond the professional-sports industry! Companies are developing their own mascots!* Perhaps a few of the students are momentarily pushing aside MBA plans in favor of the prancing and pratfalls business. A few approach Schoenewald after class.

When we return to Schoenewald's school, which is actually located in his cozy one-bedroom apartment, Schoenewald gets down to the business of making me mascot material. The constant lesson of his lectures is passion. It's a virtue that, over the next three days, he'll tirelessly trumpet. Repeatedly, he preaches his disdain for "walkabouts," costumed characters who limit themselves to glad-handing fans, à la Mickey Mouse at Disney World, and are paid minimum wage. In Schoenewald's mind, the fans come to see the mascot. The game is secondary. "When I'm in the arena," he blares repeatedly, "it's *my* house!"

Then, he tells me what I have to do to make it as a mascot.

When you're in uniform, you are the character! When the character is in the crowd, the character should always keep moving, looking for the next fan

*to mingle with! Always acknowledge the kids and the ladies! Always acknowl-
edge the ladies! Ignore the men! Never stop giving! And never stop surprising!*

Eventually, Schoenewald asks for skit ideas. What would I do as a
mascot that's new and different? I'm stumped, at least initially. When
I finally propose that my character in-line skate off a ramp and dunk a
basketball, Schoenewald retorts sharply, "Where's the surprise?" A skit
that I dub "The White Man Can't Jump Tribute" in which a preselected
guy, dressed in geeky attire, is magically (via flashing fluorescent lights
and the *Twilight Zone* theme song) transformed into a dunking god elicits barely a shrug from Schoenewald. Instead, he proposes stunts that
he has successfully performed: throwing the other team's equipment in
a dump truck . . . or being lowered from the top of the arena on a three-
wheeler . . . or running over a Barney doll with a three-wheeler. Now,
that, he exclaims, is entertainment!

The remainder of our training consists of a few physical drills: throwing and catching a football, some juggling and balancing tricks, plus I
show off my in-line skating acumen. All the while, Schoenewald preaches
passion and more passion.

Eventually, Schoenewald gets down to placement. He says that he's
constantly being contacted by teams looking for new talent, and he
gladly steers his graduates toward them. During my visit, Schoenewald
introduces me to the owner of the minor-league Nashville Sounds, floats
the prospect of a position with an NHL expansion team, mentions a
spot with the Padres, and talks up the Mr. Met position. Finally, after
the completion of my three-day boot camp, I'm released from mascot
school—with a handshake.

———

Weeks later, unexpectedly, I get a call from Schoenewald, and he declares
that I'm ready for my mascot final exam: working an actual game. As
part of my training, Schoenewald flies me out to Grand Rapids, Michigan, to be part of his mascot troupe, Gorilla Warfare, a gang of brightly
colored gorillas that perform amusing acts between hockey periods.
Schoenewald's signature crowd pleaser is running over Barney with a
three-wheeler.

For my mascot debut, about ten thousand fans are assembled at the Van Andel Arena to attend a minor-league hockey game of their beloved Griffins. I can't see a single one of them, though. Dressed in a neon-pink gorilla costume, I'm packed like a sardine with two other apes inside the belly of a Zamboni. There's not much space to move, much less breathe. My synthetic, furry costume clings to my sweat-soaked skin. As the Zamboni starts to move, I'm thinking of the Carolina Hurricanes mascot who suffered a seizure attempting the very same stunt the previous year. I feel like I'm in a skating coffin, attending my own burial at a hockey game. As the Zamboni rolls out into the blacked-out arena, my costumed cohorts and I are silent, anxiously waiting.

Fortunately, we're not waiting long. Within moments after going onto the ice, the Zamboni opens its trunk, dumping out me, my cohorts, and our bags of bananas. As I slide out, I duck my head down to avoid hitting it on the Zamboni's mouth. Although my head makes it out unscathed, my knee bangs the ice when I land. With ten thousand faces peering down at me under the glare of the arena's lights, I ignore the pain. As we had rehearsed, I run across the arena—no easy task when swaddled in an oversized gorilla costume with a molded rubber head that often covers my eyes. With everything I have, I thrust T-shirts into the mass of humanity. Barely able to see, I just keep chucking. For whatever it's worth, I'm demonstrating my athletic prowess, or lack thereof, in a professional arena.

The rest of the night is a blur. I disperse into the crowd, playing with kids and dancing with ladies and *only* ladies—until it's time for our second routine, a tried-and-true Schoenewald favorite. In this routine, my fellow gorillas invade the visitors' bench, only to discover such indiscreet objects as lingerie, which had been discreetly planted earlier in the evening. My cohorts furiously toss them onto the ice until an enraged referee—yours truly decked out in zebra garb—skates in and attempts to put an end to their antics. Without missing a beat, Gorilla Schoenewald and I get up in each other's faces, raising our arms and screaming at the top of our lungs like former Baltimore Orioles manager Earl Weaver used to do with umpires. After going at it for thirty seconds or so, Schoenewald points his right arm, my cue to turn around, so that the other gorillas can douse me with huge buckets of water. I play it big to the packed house, screaming in shock. Sure, it was cold, but I can't feel it. As Thespians like to say, I am in the moment.

———

After my Grand Rapids stint, I stay in touch with Schoenewald, who intrigues me. Eventually, I interview him. By now, there's a familiarity between us and he lets his guard down. Schoenewald is a mascot, but he's *not* always that warm and fuzzy. He's intense, and he doesn't shy away from four-letter words.

Schoenewald's story began in Ocean City, New Jersey, just outside Atlantic City, where he was one of eight children and his family scrimped to get by. "We were poor, real poor," Schoenewald recalled. "We got creative to survive." In fact, Schoenewald said that he dove into Salvation Army bins and went through fields to pick vegetables that had not yet been harvested.

As a youngster, Schoenewald dreamed of becoming a star athlete. His mother, who worked as babysitter for some of the wives of the Philadelphia Phillies, hit ground balls to him on the front lawn and gave him a dime for every ball that he put out in Little League. Schoenewald was practically without fault in the field, but his father was not as smooth. Convicted of counterfeiting, he did two years in Lewisburg state prison. "I thought everybody's dad was in prison," Schoenewald recalled with a melancholy laugh.

In high school, Schoenewald acted in summer stock theater and played sports. He planned on attending college in North Dakota, where he hoped to make the hockey team as a walk-on. However, at the last minute, he decided to skip school and become a mascot. Schoenewald took his college savings of $1,200, purchased a costume, and offered his services to the Eagles. "They said no thanks, but they also said we can't stop you," he recalled. Undeterred, Schoenewald showed up at Veterans Stadium as "Birdbrain" and was quickly embraced. His finest moment came during a Monday Night Football game in Dallas, when an inebriated Cowboys fan lit Schoenewald's left wing on fire. Schoenewald was never formally recognized or compensated by the Eagles organization, and he got by doing speaking engagements. However, he felt he was destined for greater things.

It was in San Jose where Schoenewald caused perhaps his greatest stir. After a two-day tryout, San Jose hired Schoenewald to be their Shark, making him the NHL's first-ever official mascot. By exiting the mouth of a Zamboni and bungee jumping, Schoenewald garnered attention, by his own account earning four CNN plays of the day. "I came in unannounced, uninvited, and stole the show!" boasted Schoenewald. "You can't do much better than I did in San Jose. And I'm talking Chicken-, Phanatic-level stuff. They never went the places the Shark went as far as holding the crowd in their hand." San Francisco columnist Rob Morse agreed, writing that "Schoenewald is to the Sharks what Bobby Orr is to the Boston Bruins—the star of the show." Schoenewald was in the limelight, but he believes that all the publicity ruffled some feathers within Sharks management. "You gotta imagine that it irked some people," said Schoenewald. "After they've worked for months, fifteen-hour days, this clown comes in from New Jersey and steals the show in a goofy furry costume." The tension reached a boiling point when a Sharks female executive, a former accomplished figure skater, complained that Schoenewald's skating wasn't up to snuff. Promptly, an ice-skating rink was rented, and Schoenewald was forced to showcase his grace. "She wanted me to skate like a swan!" recalled Schoenewald. "She said 'do this' and she did a swan thing. I'm working in front of an NHL crowd that goes wild over fights. They do not want a swan. Kiss my royal ass!"

Soon enough, Schoenewald was out of San Jose.

So he skated right over to the Ottawa Senators. Once again, Schoenewald planned to work the crowd into a frenzy, to be worth the price of admission. However, the Canadian government was not prepared for such plans. Schoenewald said the Senators failed to obtain work visas for any of its employees, including their players—and mascot. Desperate to make an impact, missing opening night was not an option for Schoenewald. To make the debut game, Schoenewald said that he rented a pedal boat and pedaled across the St. Lawrence River, using a hockey stick as a rudder. In Ottawa, Schoenewald once again provoked controversy. Specifically, women's groups were offended by his Michael Jackson routine, in which he mimicked the gloved one (with his lion's head on) and had a horde of provocatively dressed waitresses tear off his pull-away costume, only to reveal Schoenewald in a flesh body suit. When Schoenewald lit a bonfire on the ice, a fire marshal was waiting for him in the locker room. Soon after, Schoenewald was out of Ottawa.

The very next season, Schoenewald came home to Jersey. He said that he negotiated a six-figure-plus salary for himself with the New Jersey Devils general manager Lou Lamoriello. Once again, Schoenewald was up to his antics. He danced like James Brown with a nun (Schoenewald's then girlfriend) and shot three Disney dolls out on to the ice the first time the Mighty Ducks played the Devils. Soon after, though, the homecoming went sour. Night after night, fans yelled derisive remarks at him, stuff like "Stay away from my wife!" Schoenewald was baffled, until he was informed that the previous Devils' mascot had been accused of inappropriately touching women. Furious at Lamoriello for not informing him of his predecessor's misbehavior, Schoenewald needled the general manager by wearing opposing teams' jerseys into the office. "I went out and bought a Canadiens jersey and I can't stand the Canadiens!" he said. Ultimately, in Schoenewald's mind, at least, Lamoriello got his revenge, ordering Schoenewald to shoot promotional T-shirts into the crowd with a rubber band. Schoenewald protested this stunt vigorously, declaring it bush league. He saw himself as an entertainer, the game merely an intermission for his act. Grimacing, Schoenewald played the good soldier and shot the T-shirts into the crowd. One of the shirts, however, sailed into the upper deck, and an overzealous fan nearly fell off the balcony grasping for it. After the game, Schoenewald was summoned to Lamoriello's inner sanctum, where the rubber band was sitting on his desk like an official court document. According to Schoenewald, Lamoriello told him in no uncertain terms that shooting T-shirts into the upper deck was strictly forbidden and ordered him to continue shooting T-shirts into the crowd, just not the top tier. Once again, a now livid Schoenewald resisted. And once again, he was overruled. This time, Schoenewald fought back. "Now they have a popular mascot that's bringing down the house every night, and I have got to use those stupid fuckin' rubber bands for only a couple of hundred bucks that they're getting out of some goofy company," bristled Schoenewald, his voice rising. "And now I'm not allowed to shoot them into the upper deck? Fuck you! The way I say fuck you is clean out my house and shoot all twelve of them in the upper deck. Fuck you! One of them hit the top of the stadium!"

Immediately after that, Schoenewald was out of Jersey and on to Nashville . . . to teach mascot wannabes.

————

A few years after my mascot debut, Schoenewald moved on to women's tackle football. But after a three-day, tumultuous stint as the commissioner of the Nashville Women's Football League, Schoenewald was on the road again, where we reconnected. "I'm like a homeless person with potential," he said with a somber laugh. "I've had money. I've had no money. It does not matter to me either way." Eventually, Schoenewald landed in Denver, where he became the commissioner of a new women's professional league, the United Women's Football League, one of the dozens of women's tackle football leagues that had popped up around the country. Schoenewald came up with a unique marketing strategy. He said that the league had set up a plan with the Denver Public Schools and that kids would be admitted free to the games, which would be played at Denver's Invesco Field (now Sports Authority Field). Schoenewald said that the atmosphere of the games would be football, Willy Wonka style. He promised balloons, games, refreshments, and, yes, mascots. "A League of Their Own had nothing," said Schoenewald as he drove down Interstate 25 alone in his car. "This is a winner!"

————

While Schoenewald appeared to be moving on to brighter pastures, I wasn't quite done with mascot work. After answering an ad at the suggestion of a colleague, I eventually become a Newark Bear, the mascot for an independent league baseball team. I land the gig for three reasons, not necessarily in this order:

1. I laud my Mascot Mania handshake.
2. They're paying practically nothing.
3. And last, perhaps most important, apparently no one else wants the gig.

So in my bear suit, I walk around an elementary school, wave to kids, and basically act goofy. I can certainly handle this job. However, I don't really want to. When you're a mascot, you can't talk, and you sweat like you're in the Sahara. Worst of all, somewhat tragically, I have become what Schoenewald detests: a "walkabout," the absolute lowest form of mascot. Ultimately, my *other*, non-costumed work just wouldn't permit me to stay on with the Bears—and that's a good thing. Ecstatic to never wear the bear suit again, I swear that I won't be uncomfortable in my own skin.

5

Invisible at the U.S. Open

It's Judgment Day as far as whether or not I make it as a U.S. Open ball person. When I show up for my tryout at a public court just outside the U.S. Open facility in Flushing Meadows, New York, I'm already sweating. It's July, unusually hot and muggy and fifth-set-tie-break tense. Standing at the net, the Ball Czar, a tall, lean authoritative woman in tennis whites and shades, is very much in charge. When it's my turn, the Czar directs me to a corner of the court, and a kid, probably sixteen, is directed to my side's other corner. An older woman, probably the Kid's mother, stands off to the side.

The Kid and I are across from each other. In front of us, one of the Czar's underlings, Racket Man, stands at the net, holding a racket and a handful of balls. As I wait, perspiring, the Czar lays out her agenda: when she gives the command, Racket Man's gonna smash a ball into the back fence, directly into the middle portion of the court. (John McEnroe, or Johnny Mac, a former Open ball person, refers to this area as no-man's-land because it's an area of the court that's not assigned to a particular ball person. Hit there, it's *anyone's* ball.) Once the ball enters no-man's-land, the Kid and I are supposed to race after it. Whoever gets to it first will scoop it up and we'll both return to our respective corners—one of us empty-handed. So there's two of us, and there's one ball and one winner. It's a race to the ball. It's mano a mano. I mean mano a kiddo.

Finally, the Czar nods. Promptly, Racket Man slams the ball and it ricochets off the fence. Momentarily, I'm taken aback by the slam's force and before taking off, I wait to see where the ball hits. Big mistake. In a blink, the Kid has the ball and is running back to his corner. I barely got off the block.

It's 15-Love in favor of the Kid.

It wasn't so much that I lost. It was *how* I lost. He easily beat me to the ball, which had landed just barely on *my* side of the court.

I practically limp back to my corner, empty-handed, perspiring more than ever. Worse, I'm sucking wind. Instead of practicing throws for this tryout, I should've been doing sprints. I'm also getting my ass kicked by someone who just had their braces removed. Actually, for all I know, he might still have his braces on. This punk's making me look old—ancient, actually. In the Kid's world, I'm a relic, practically Smithsonian material!

———

As I wait in the corner for the Czar's next command, I ponder the road I took to get to this point. About five years earlier, it started with a classified ad asking for U.S. Open ball persons. Immediately, I thought that this was something I *needed* to do. If I couldn't make it at the Open as a player, I would get there as a ball person. So in the early summer, I showed up for the open tryout, where hundreds of kids and very young adults were assembled. Eventually, I ran in front of the net, scooping up balls as evaluators scrutinized my every move, taking copious notes. I threw balls across the length of the court. Besides momentarily fumbling a ball at the net, I nailed the audition, certainly good enough to get the $7.75-per-hour gig. They'd be in touch, or so they said. Days after the tryout, I heard nothing.

A few weeks later, I received this form letter:

> Dear Prospective Ball Person,
>
> Thank you for your interest in being a U.S. Open Ball Person. As of this time, all positions have been filled. We will keep your information on file until August 14 in the event an opening becomes available.
>
> Sincerely,
> Tina Taps
> U.S. Open Director of Ball Persons

Yes, Tina Taps is her real name, and yes, that is her real title, and yes, it was a firm rejection. Officially, I was a ball person reject.

I didn't give up. The very next day, I got Taps on the phone and passionately petitioned for another shot, claiming that an egregious error had been made. Surprisingly, she granted me another tryout. Unfortunately, I was in Newport, Rhode Island, covering the X Games, and couldn't make it. Thus, I remained a ball person reject.

———

Fast forward five years, and I was at a crossroads. My steady copywriting gig had disappeared, and I caught wind that ball person tryouts were about to take place. Once again, I made my way to Flushing Meadows. This time, there were even more prospects. On one of the outer courts, I sat in the bleachers with a few hundred other wannabes. Before the actual tryouts began, there was a formal introduction by Taps. Right after the U.S. Open Director of Ball Persons began speaking, she was rudely interrupted.

"You cannot be serious!" someone yelled from the stands. "You cannot be serious!"

Everyone looked around, stunned. Who could be so rude as to actually interrupt the U.S. Open Director of Ball Persons?

It turned out it was one of ESPN's broadcasters—Kenny Mayne, I think—attempting to mimic a memorable Johnny Mac rant. I'd learn later that ESPN was doing a segment on the ball person tryouts.

When it was my turn, I hustled through the audition process. This time around, my pickups were without fault, and I threw the balls with a little extra pace, making certain that they hit the intended target on one hop as the Open requires. No problem. I have a very strong arm—at least compared to adolescents. Still, I thought I might need help in the selection process. I got the sense that my advanced age in the ball person universe might be a major issue, perhaps even a deal breaker. Unfortunately, I was way past my ball person prime. I was older than many of the players. So, frankly, if I didn't earn a ball person spot now, I probably wasn't gonna make it at all. It was do or die. I put in a Hail Mary call to my friend, the Player, who knows a lot of people, including a lot of ball people in high places. The Player agreed to put in a word for me. He made no promises, but I didn't want any. If I'm good enough, let me run balls out for balls. If I suck, brand me a ball person reject for life.

I kept anxiously checking my mail. This time, instead of a thin, form rejection letter, I got an invitation for yet *another* tryout. I was pleased, but I was feeling the pressure. So I started training. Early mornings, I practiced my throws against a wall in a school yard. I did sprints. In an attempt to make a positive impression, I even purchased a new shirt and shorts.

=====

As I'm recalling an abbreviated version of this, I notice Ball Mom out of the corner of my eye. She's beaming with pride. It's not fair: the Kid has a cheering section. Anyway, this triggers something in me. Johnny Mac's signature phrase keeps bouncing around inside of me: *You cannot be serious!* I'm silently screaming at myself, attempting to psyche myself up. Down 15-Love, I must pick myself off the canvas. Now, the goal has changed. It's not so much about the ball person position but about saving face. If either is going to happen, I must find my wheels. Unfortunately, the Kid is quicker than I am. Just like Johnny Mac, I'm throwing myself over the coals. *I'm a disgrace!* As I struggle to hide my hyperventilation, I vow that my young nemesis will not get any balls on my side. This is it! No more slow starts. No more excuses. There's no tomorrow! If I have to, I'll tackle the Kid, rip the ball out of his hands, and send him back to his orthodontist. Let his momma come after me. Let's get it on!

And we do. Repeatedly, ball after ball after ball is rocketed into no-man's-land. I grit my teeth as my feet somehow find that faster gear. I'm in the zone. Ball Mom's smile disappears. I keep my vow and even get a couple of balls that are on the Kid's side. *Take that.* Alas, a cease-fire is ordered and the ball onslaught comes to a halt. As I stand in my corner soaked, the Czar carefully looks over my application.

"So you're available to work every day?" she finally asks.

As I attempt to catch my breath, I seriously contemplate this question.

Is this an actual job offer, or is it a trick question? If I'm too available, that might work against me. Perhaps I shouldn't be *so* available.

Ultimately, I opt for the truth.

"I can work every day," I respond. If the Czar asks me to work every match, I will. I'm ready.

"Are you on vacation?" she asks in her no-nonsense tone.

"No."

It's official: I'm being interrogated. Johnny Mac's other signature phrase, which he had rifled at many an umpire during his career, is now bouncing around inside my head courtesy of the Czar: *Answer the Question!*

"You're unemployed!?" the Czar snaps. This strikes a sensitive nerve because I'm still reeling from the disappearance of my copywriting gig.

"I'm freelance!" I blurt back awkwardly after a seeming eternity, almost apologetically. "I have a flexible schedule!"

You could fill a small swimming pool with my perspiration.

After jotting down a few notes, the Czar finally excuses me from the witness stand—uh, my corner—and directs me to the side of the court for phase two of the tryout. She asks me to throw the ball across the entire length of the court just as I've done during my previous auditions. At the other Grand Slams—the French, Wimbledon, and Australian—ball persons aren't required to make this somewhat monumental throw. Instead, balls are transferred from one side of the court to the other via an assembly line, with ball persons at the back of the court rolling the balls to their brethren at the net, who in turn roll the balls to the other end of the court. At the Open, it's just one enchilada, one throw. Perhaps because of the trauma of my battle with the Kid, the throw seems much longer. Unfortunately, I can barely make out who I'm throwing the ball to because of the sun's glare and the sweat that's partially blinding me. When the Czar gives the signal, I launch ball after ball forcefully but not too forcefully to the other side of the court, again on one bounce. Ultimately, I acquit myself well. Still, I wonder if it's enough. The pressure is getting to me. Again, this is my last chance: if I don't make the cut this time, I'll never pick up balls at the U.S. Open. Taking no chances, I prod the Player into making another call on my behalf, though I'm nervous about what he'll hear back. My fears are completely unfounded. Apparently the Czar was impressed with my arm strength and simply refers to me as "the guy with the arm."

Within days, I get another letter, not thin, not thick. It tells me when to report and includes a long list of ball person rules and regulations. Here are most of them:

- Each ball person crew has a leader, who is referred to as a crew chief.
- Bring a beverage to the court. On the court, supplies are limited. Drink plenty of fluids.
- Arrive at the court in full uniform. Never dress or undress on the court.
- Ball persons positioned in the back of the court should assist players with their warm-ups.
- In extreme heat, rotate every twenty-five minutes.
- Balls should always be on the server's end of the court. During a tiebreaker, opposite ends keep two balls.
- The back ball persons on the server's end should always share their balls.
- Hold your position until the point is over.
- Always signal to the other ball persons when you are ready to throw or receive.
- Hold your hands at shoulder level to show server whether or not you have balls.
- Wait for server to motion before tossing to them. When they signal, take a step toward them and toss them the ball on one bounce. Do not throw balls under any circumstances between first and second serves.
- Be careful where you stand. Do not block scoreboard or signage.
- Do not lean on the fence or juggle balls.
- The main goal is to get the ball off the court as quickly and efficiently as possibly, so play can resume.

It finished with this message:

> Ball persons are constantly evaluated by umpires, referees, ball person supervisors, and scorers. Do your best at all times.

Remember, this is America's Grand Slam Event! Being a U.S. Open ball person is a very big responsibility and YOU are an integral part of the success of the tournament. Have pride in your work. Remember every court is a U.S. Open court. Even Sampras and Hingis started off on the field courts. If you do a great job, show athletic talent, and have a good, enthusiastic attitude, you will be asked to do a feature match. ALWAYS BE COURTEOUS! UNIFORM NEAT, CLEAN AND WORN PROPERLY!

A week later, I report to the ball person war room, the Perch, which is between Louis Armstrong Court and the Grandstand, the Open's second and third largest courts. The granddaddy of courts, Arthur Ashe Stadium, a 23,000-seat behemoth, is just next door. In the center of the Perch, atop a concrete platform, the Czar stands in front of an enormous magnetic whiteboard. She's constantly moving around magnets on the board, each representing a different ball person. The Czar is constantly strategizing about where she should position her charges. Her finest will work where the cameras are, otherwise known as the "television courts" or "features courts." Armstrong, the Grandstand, Ashe, and a small handful of outer courts are television courts.

As I'm mentally preparing myself to run and throw in front of, well, the world, I get some horrendous news: I'm *not* an official ball person. I've only made the Open's qualifying tournament. Known as the Qualies, it's a pre-tournament, a tournament before the actual tournament for mostly relative unknowns who haven't earned enough tour points to automatically qualify for the tourney's Main Draw. If a player wins three matches in the Qualies, they earn an invitation to the Main Draw. Unfortunately for me, the Czar still needs to cut some people, and I have to prove myself and then some to advance to the Main Draw. I desperately want to advance because working the Qualies doesn't make me an official U.S. Open ball person. If I don't make the Main Draw, well, this entire episode was one big mishit. I'm not out of the woods.

Compared to the Main Draw, the Qualies are minor league. In the Qualies, there's no admission fee, all matches are two out of three sets (instead of five, at least for the men), and many of the Main Draw's fancy bells and whistles are missing. There are no ushers at the exits, so fans can come and go as they please between points. As for the ball people, we're given U.S. Open ball person jerseys but no other portion of the uniform. Immediately, my mission becomes landing the rest of the outfit. However, this might not happen. Standing atop her platform, the Czar looks down at us with a dead-serious expression and repeatedly warns that many of us—she cryptically doesn't specify how many exactly—will not make the Main Draw. The Czar says that she's looking for weaknesses in her fleet and will take only the finest and fittest. Nervously, I stare at a throng of high school kids, attempting to gauge if they have the goods to take my spot.

After all this, I'm *still* trying out.

On the first day of the Qualies, I'm fired up for my debut on Court 18. I'm ready to show off my skills to the Czar, not to mention the fans. When I arrive, though, Court 18 is a virtual ghost town: no cameras, no people—but lots of pollen and insects. As far as courts, Court 18 is practically Siberia, located at the edge of the Grand Slam's grounds. As we wait for the players, our six-person ball person squad stands in a line at the front of the entrance. I'm not calm. One of my colleagues, a twelve-year-old veteran Net—one of the ball persons who runs after balls in front of the net—can't ignore my tense demeanor. "Don't be nervous," he tells me. After the players enter, we wait in our linear formation for them to reach their chairs. When the second player places his bag down, we break out of our line and run to our prearranged positions. This ball person practice is called the Burst. As far as I know, the Burst is an American innovation, as none of the other Slams perform it. After a flawless burst, the match plays out just fine, and just as I'm starting to feel confident, the aforementioned Net points out that I've broken one of the cardinal rules: I've partially blocked one of the corporate sponsor's letters on the back fence. This is an infraction. Just like Johnny Mac, I grimace in disgust. Never, ever again.

After a few matches, I find my inner ball person. When you're a ball person, you're not *in* the match. But you're *into* the match, watching it intently, tracking every point. Basically, you have to be aware of everything that's happening and about to happen. If a ball person spaces out, which is surprisingly easy to do, he or she will be gone, as the Czar keeps warning us. Each Back—a ball person who stands at the back of the court—on the server's side should have two balls at all times so the server has quick, easy access. So throughout the matches, between points, of course, there's a silent game going on. Balls are constantly rotating to ensure that each Back on the server's side has two balls. Some female players request one ball at a time, which is an obvious mental adjustment for ball persons. As a Back, I'm constantly flashing my hands, letting my on-court colleagues know how many balls I have and if I need any. Every match, I'm basically playing a game of catch with my five other court mates. Atop her perch, the Czar often gazes down at the action on the Grandstand and Armstrong Courts, nodding her approval—not at the play of the players but at the smooth ball rotation of her ball persons. The best ball persons are seemingly invisible, facilitating the match so that it proceeds seamlessly. The worst are the ones who provide a distraction or interrupt the match in some way, such as hitting an umpire (made front page news) or a player (occurred during the Qualies and remained under the radar) with an errant throw.

Every odd game, the players switch sides and break for a few minutes, but ball persons get no rest. Guess who gets to hold the umbrella? And it's not just holding the umbrella. It's tilting it at just the right angle, so that it shields the player from any hint of sunlight. After the match's last point, ball persons are forbidden to move until the players shake hands. During my two-hour shifts, I talk to no one. In late August heat, I hustle hard for desperate, qualifying-round players. I'm just about as desperate as they are. We all share the same goal: the Main Draw.

Just about all of the players in the Qualies are unknowns. Arnaud Clement, a onetime finalist in the Australian Open, is the exception, and his reputation for being temperamental precedes him. Formerly a top-ten player, Clement isn't pleased about having to play the Qualies. Actually, Clement is running late and everyone, from the ball persons to the umpire to the crowd, wonders if he's going to show at all. After some calls are made, Clement appears. His match is not a walk, and Clement seems annoyed at the amount of effort that he's being forced to expend, not to mention the constant fan traffic. Several times, the umpire, who is also auditioning for a spot in the Main Draw, informs Clement that the Qualies have a no-usher policy and that he's just going to have to cope. While Clement is nothing but a gentleman to me, my colleagues aren't so fortunate. "Go back to your corner," Clement barks in his heavy accent at a ball person who innocently stepped a few feet toward him as he short tossed him a ball to serve. Apparently, Clement's in the *zone*, a sweet spot of concentration, and he wants his space. After a set, it's clear: Clement is overwhelmingly anal. He folds his bandana wide around his forehead, has his special bottles (of water, I presume) wrapped in a separate plastic bag, and often likes to inspect the fabric of the balls before serving as if one ball might provide an advantage over the other. Perhaps Clement believes one ball has more bounce. Clement isn't the only player who is particularly picky about their balls. If the server hits a winner with a certain ball, he or she often requests that specific ball again. Sometimes, in a quest for the best possible ball, players methodically examine all of the balls before settling on two.

As temperatures often exceed a hundred degrees on court, at least during the early days of the tournament, players and ball persons alike crave shade. In an attempt to stay cool and perhaps catch a breather, players wave me off, go deep in *my* corner, and fetch their own towel, leaving me standing around feeling somewhat superfluous and foolish. *I want to hand off the damn towel!* Unlike the vast majority of the players, Clement wears sunglasses. Not surprisingly, ball persons aren't allowed to wear shades. However, we're mandated to rotate out of the glare. If we don't, there are often dire consequences. It's not uncommon for ball persons to actually faint mid-match. One year, in the span of just a few hot days, as many as six ball persons fainted during matches. Unfortunately, today, our crew chief, the leader of our six-person squad, hasn't mentioned a rotation. Perhaps he's nervous that Clement, a routine freak like many of the players, might go ballistic if we change positions. In all likelihood, though, he selfishly just wants to stay out of the sun. Or perhaps even more likely, he just forgot. Wilting, I'm not convinced that I'm impressing the ball person evaluators who are roaming the grounds, scrutinizing performances. During a changeover, I steal a look at one of their grading sheets, which has these categories:

ARM
SPEED
APPEARANCE
AGILITY
HANDS

What's the toughest part of the job, at least for me?

Stopping.

After running five yards, stopping on a dime is surprisingly taxing. I attempt to be the perfect ball person, finding the perfect balance between all-out exertion and motionless stoicism.

After some tense moments, Clement takes control of the match. Put aside his sometimes difficult mood, he's easy to root for. Only 5-foot-8, Clement is not going to overpower anyone, so he has to beat you with craftiness and persistence. As it becomes clear that Clement will advance, his mood brightens. Suddenly the fan traffic is non-existent. At the conclusion, the once-brusque Frenchman finds his joie de vivre and signs autographs for the admission-free crowd.

While Clement finds his form, I discover that mine needs improvement. During a break, an evaluator pulls me aside and critiques my arm. "You've got a nice arm," says Jeff, a tennis coach. "Now, I want to see darts."

Later, I learned that Jeff was just having fun with me.

However, another evaluator appears to be dead serious, and she takes exception with my short toss to the server, pointing out that it's "intimidating." Immediately, I soften my short toss, trying something that feels unnatural. As I see it, my short toss is not a toss at all. It's actually a flick.

In the midst of the Qualies, I try to figure out which way the Czar is leaning as far as keeping me, questioning her underlings about my chances. Everyone is poker-faced. I'm on edge, in a ball person zone, obsessed with running after balls. I desperately want to move on to the Main Draw. By the end of the third day, I'm spent. If the Czar cuts me now, there'll be no regrets. I left it all out on the court.

On the last day of the Qualies, the Czar doesn't assign me to a court. Instead, she directs me to an office in the bowels of the stadium. As I walk downstairs, I'm prepared for the worst: to receive my walking papers and be branded a ball boy reject for life.

Instead, an underling hands me a clear plastic bag. Slowly, I open it. I can breathe easy.

There are the official U.S. Open shorts, sneakers, socks, as well as an uncomfortable, ill-fitting warm-up suit that I'll never, ever wear.

It's official: I made it to the Main Draw.

There's not a moment of celebration, though. The Czar doesn't allow me or any of my brethren to get comfortable. She wants us to keep hustling hard, so she continues to chide us for infractions, however small, and threatens termination. The Czar says that we're lucky, explaining that the Open is "camp" compared to Wimbledon, where ball persons are sequestered and not allowed to roam the grounds between shifts as we are. Indeed, the ball persons have it good at the Open. We get a $15 allowance that we can use at the Open's famously expensive food court during our breaks.

On the first day of the Main Draw, the crowds arrive in droves. Once again, I'm banished to the Open's Siberia: Courts 17 and 18. On these very courts, though, I work a memorable match, a marathon that goes well past the day session and into the evening. Before about maybe forty spectators, under the lights, two relative unknowns slug it out into the fifth set. A feisty Frenchman by the name of Slimane Saoudi is giving fits to favorite Ivo Heuberger. "He hasn't won anything!" mutters Heuberger after a particularly frustrating point. Heuberger is just about right, at least by elite professional athletes' standards. For the year, Saoudi had made less than $16,000 in tournament earnings. Now, more than money is at stake. Winning a Grand Slam match can validate an entire career. Unfortunately for Heuberger, Saoudi is on the brink of taking this match—that is, if he doesn't collapse first. During the crucial fifth set, a medical aide is called to the court to massage Saoudi's limbs. The Frenchman lies down on the court in a hypnotic state, attempting to muster the strength to continue. Meanwhile, Heuberger battles mental demons. At one point, he hurls his racket at the fence in frustration. The racket comes precariously close to hitting a linesman, who shifts his head at the last moment. After this reckless act, the court becomes eerily silent. I'm standing about five or so yards away. What's next? Is Heuberger gonna start chucking objects at the guy who fetches his towel?

It wasn't the only time that I shared an unpleasant encounter with a player. Unforgettably, Russian-American Alex Bogomolov, a player who's probably better known for his friendship with former female player Anna Kournikova than his on-court game, retreats to my corner where there's a nice piece of shade. Then, without warning or provocation, he spits a startling large wad of saliva against the fence, mere inches from where I'm standing. Since this is unchartered territory, I'm not sure what to do. I probably should've run for cover. Instead, I firmly stand my ground, refusing to give an inch. Right after his spit smacks the fence, Bogomolov and I momentarily watch the moisture cascade down. Fortunately, it didn't hit the sponsor's sacred signage. It just might be Bogomolov's best shot of the match, and I desperately want to tell him that. Of course, ball persons are not allowed to talk to the players. Instead, I convey this thought to Bogomolov with a quick glance: *You're out of your mind if you think I'm gonna clean that up!*

But even if I insisted, even if I petitioned, I couldn't clean up Bogomolov's spit. Bodily fluids are strictly off limits to ball persons. Once, after a player became ill and tossed his cookies, ball persons cleaned up the mess, but consequently the Czar firmly forbade any similar acts, explaining that this was the domain of the court attendants, the court's custodians. Court attendants and ball persons are the equivalent of church and state. I speculate the Czar's rationale was that she didn't want the ball person to get any vomit on the balls. Very understandable.

As the Saoudi-Heuberger match heads to the fifth set tiebreaker, the combatants continue to pace (often in *my* corner) as they mutter to themselves something that will inspire them to make it to the promised land: the Second Round. After the racquet throwing incident, Heuberger seems somewhat embarrassed and repentant, whispering "Thank you" each time I throw him a ball or hand him his towel. He's fortunate that his racket didn't harm the line judge and transform him from an unknown pro to international headline. Strangely, I empathize with Heuberger's breakdown. Once or twice, I've come to the brink of losing my mind on court. During a few women's singles rallies, which go back and forth and on and on and on at moderate to slow speed, at least compared to the men's, I want to rudely interrupt and put an abrupt end to these gruntathons. *Hit the damn ball into the net already! I got a job to do! I got a ball to run after and fetch!*

Ultimately, Heuberger advances.

Late in the Main Draw's first week, I land a plum assignment, a men's single match on the Grandstand, one of the televised, stadium courts. It's more than just a mere third-round match. It's a homecoming and somewhat of a coronation. On the slate is American up-and-comer James Blake, whom many tout as the next great American champion. An hour or so before the match, though, the Grandstand is in serious peril. Earlier in the day, it had been pouring, and now water is seeping down from the stands and onto the court. Rain delays are no fun for anyone, especially ball persons. Besides the Perch or the tiny, subterranean ball person locker room, there's nowhere to go and not much to do except wait, spend the $15 per diem (which will only stretch so far), and watch old matches, which the Open plays on its jumbotrons. Once in a while, viewing old matches can be fun. When longtime veteran ball person Gary Spitz, the Don Budge of ball persons, watches the memorable 1991 Jimmy Connors and Aaron Krickstein third rounder that he worked, he does a roll call of that match's ball persons. In addition to Spitz, who now mostly serves in an administrative capacity, there are a handful of ball persons who are in their thirties or even forties. For the most part, the older ball persons stay in the shadows, relegated to the outer courts or administrative duties.

Fortunately, this rain delay is not too long. However, the resident court dryers are unavailable for the Grandstand, probably busy on other courts, so I take matters into my own hands. I towel off the water that's crept onto the Grandstand with a laundry bag full of towels. With the water gone, the much-anticipated third-round match gets underway. As expected, the crowd of about five thousand (my estimate) is firmly behind Blake, applauding his every winner and bemoaning each of his misfires. Working in front of a large vocal crowd is a rush. Long, cross-court throws are effortless. In the Grandstand, an intimate arena where it feels as if the fans are right on top of you, it's not unusual for spectators to attempt to strike up a conversation. "I want to see that on one hop," a fan tells me good-naturedly. (No, I don't disappoint.) In fact, I hurl that ball like a javelin, delivering a rope. Forgive the boast. Understand, I'm a ball person closing in on social security!

Though it's a distraction, it's fun when the spectators get involved. Australian fans are the house rowdies, the equivalent of Yankee Stadium's Bleacher Creatures, though the Aussies always seem to be good-natured. Shirtless, flag waving, face-painted, Heineken swigging, the Aussies sing Men at Work songs and other stuff at every opportunity. In tribute to a fellow Aussie, Samantha Stosur, they come up with this: *When Sammy rocks the court . . . When Sammy rocks the court . . . When Sammy rocks the court . . . She rocks it all night long!*

When the Aussies aren't singing, they actually cheer the ball persons. It's much, much appreciated. Unfortunately, I've also experienced the opposite reaction. Specifically, when a non–ball person colleague, who's in the stands, spots me working a match by chance, I expect him to congratulate me on my arm strength, concentration, and overall athleticism. No such luck. "You're a man out there!" he aggressively chastises me. "You're out there with kids!" Conversely, when Newmark spots me in uniform just by chance, he doesn't bat an eye. He knows it's just business as usual for me.

I'm thoroughly enjoying the electric atmosphere of the Blake match. In an instant, though, my excitement becomes mild horror. Blake cranks a 115-mile-per-hour serve directly at me. On the small confines of the Grandstand, there's nowhere to dodge. Instead of moving, I just stand there momentarily paralyzed, and I don't get my hands up quick enough. POP! The ball smacks me in the lower abdomen—but it appears to go slightly lower. The crowd lets out a collective groan. Blake waves to me, apologizing for hitting me in the balls. But, I want to explain to Blake, to the entire crowd—to the worldwide television audience, for that matter—that I'm OK and that, well . . . *the ball didn't hit me in the balls!* Someone, anyone, please get me a microphone. Instead, I follow the ball person code to the letter and say nothing, maintaining my stoic composure, not even smiling. And to be honest, I'm not smiling because I'm not happy. Five thousand fans, not to mention an international television audience, think I just took one in the nuts! But I make it seem as if it's business as usual, just another day at the office.

After Labor Day, during the second and final week of the Open, the tone of the tournament dramatically changes. It's noticeably cooler, and there are fewer players, not to mention ball persons, many of whom have returned to school. Still, there are plenty of matches—lots of doubles, seniors, juniors, and wheelchair, which are the toughest because the pace is completely different, much slower, since two bounces are allowed. During these wheelchair duels, it's extremely tough to not space out. Juniors aren't much better. The young players fall into two categories: entitled and spoiled, or awkward and uncomfortable with ball persons serving them. I want to say this: *Don't grab the ball! Just allow to me do my job!* Meanwhile, doubles matches are a breeze. With so many players on the court, the doubles teams often take care of their own balls. After working high-intensity singles matches, all of these matches feel too easy, and I feel unnecessary, a somewhat tragic fate for any ball person. But I'm a ball person, and I go where they send me.

I work so many of the chest-bumping, doubles team Bryan Brothers matches that I feel like an honorary brother. The toughest thing about the Bryan Brothers matches is telling the two apart, which I still can't actually do. It doesn't matter, though. Very few people care about doubles, and we're almost always in an empty house. There's one person that doesn't miss a Bryan match, though: a lone, mysterious man high in the stands behind one of the service lines. He lives for the Bryan Brothers. Who is this fanatic?

Later, I learned that he's their father.

As I work my way through the grab bag of matches, I wage a private war with my allergies, which hit me hard during the Open's second week. As I stand on the court during serves, I'm often struggling to suppress a sneeze. A time or two, though, I lose this battle and let loose a violent torrent of sneezes. Such a ferocious fit occurs during a wheelchair match, which Wimbledon's Ball Czar happens to be attending, perhaps scouting talent. While my torrent was fierce and relentless, match play was surprisingly not stopped. However, and I say this with a tinge of sadness and regret, I'm not expecting an invitation to work Wimbledon anytime soon.

As the tournament winds down, I get some unexpected good news: I'm one of the finalists for ball person Rookie of the Year. Frankly, I didn't know such an award existed. Regardless, I'm honored. I'm not the quickest, and I don't possess the best hands or arm, but I've been extremely focused. Prior to this moment, I wasn't aware that I was earning high marks. Apparently, the Czar only confronts you when you mess up, or when she schedules you to work one of the finals matches. Meanwhile, at the Perch, I overhear that FBI agents are prowling the premises, some undercover. One fellow ball person comes right out and asks me if I'm on the job, citing my relatively advanced age. I feel a sense of mild outrage. It's not because he thinks that I look a little older than the average ball person. After three weeks of court time, I feel as though I'm a ball person to the core, a finalist for ball person Rookie of the Year. I don't run after fugitives. I run after balls!

———

I had worked hard to become a ball person. I couldn't quit after only one year. I felt like I had put a lifetime into becoming a Grand Slam ball person! So even though I wound up finishing second for Rookie of the Year honors, I return to Flushing Meadows the following year. Most notably, I still hadn't worked a match in Arthur Ashe Stadium. With that goal in my sights, I return to the Perch, feeling like I never left. Jeff, the aforementioned supervisor, takes a seat next to me.

"So, how was your off season?" I ask.

"Just fine," he responds. "Yours?"

"All good."

As far as conversation, that's as good as it got. I'm here to get balls, and that's it. Matches become routine, and players somewhat interchangeable, like diners to a waiter in a busy greasy spoon. I work so many female Russian matches, I feel like I should apply for a position at their embassy. Some players are unforgettable. Younes El Aynaoui, otherwise known as the Rockin' Moroccan, embraces every aspect of the Open, including the ball persons. Specifically, he's amused by how ball persons constantly rotate the balls between points. "You think this is a game," El Aynaoui comments playfully to my on-court colleague in the midst of a tense match on the Grandstand. "We'll get a beer after the match."

I don't receive the same offer.

There are other things in store for me. Between points, El Aynaoui does a mini striptease, lifting his shirt and drying his torso with his towel, which has droplets of blood on it.

Guess who gets to hold El Aynaoui's towel?

And a word about the towel: when I present the towel to the Rockin' Moroccan, I hold it up like a curtain, as I do for most of the players—but not all. Some players request that you hand them the towel in its natural state, as one big clump.

Playing on one of the outer courts, American Bethanie Mattek could definitely use a towel or two—to cover herself up. Indeed, she is the closest thing that tennis has to a Vegas show girl. Mattek sports an outlandish turquoise-and-brown cowboy hat. She wears a low-riding, bright blue mini skirt and a black polka dot bra underneath a transparent white shirt that exposes her midsection. After the first few games, an official confronts Mattek, probably about her outrageous attire. Since I'm locked in my corner position, I can't be sure. It's a long meeting and nothing seems to get resolved. Mattek doesn't put on conventional tennis whites, and she doesn't win, either, going down in straight sets.

Ilie Nastase, the 1972 U.S. Open champ from Romania, doesn't seem to care much about winning his "legends" doubles match. Nastase, who was nicknamed "Nasty" as well as "the Bucharest Buffoon" during his heyday, just wants to give the small crowd a show. During his career, Nastase was responsible for many a show. Unforgettably, he mooned an official, threw a shoe at a linesman for calling foot faults, and actually changed his clothes during a match. For my match, Nastase reverts to his old antics, heckling opponents, playing up to the ball persons—at least the female ones—and harassing linesmen ("Go home and read a Bible!"). During changeovers, Nastase talks on his cell phone. After the first few minutes, the crowd seems to lose patience for Nastase's act and starts to grumble. Ultimately, the fans just want to see tennis. Unfortunately, Nastase doesn't sense the crowd's displeasure, and he continues to play the clown card. In the end, he annoys more than entertains.

Luck of the draw, I get to see a lot of respected veteran Swede Jonas Bjorkman. Every time he enters one of the outer courts for a match, I seem to be on it, too, and we share this unspoken conversation:

ME: You again? How many times are we gonna work together?

BJORKMAN: Funny, I was going to say the exact same thing to you.

ME: You've been doing this forever! How old are you?

BJORKMAN: I was going to say the same thing to you!

But I still have yet to work the biggest court, Arthur Ashe. As a flag holder for the mixed doubles finals awards ceremony, I had been on Ashe, but that doesn't count. I'm as patriotic as the next guy, but I would've preferred to be grasping a sweaty towel during an actual match than Old Glory. Unfortunately, for whatever reason, the Czar doesn't place my magnet in the Ashe column.

Then, suddenly, one afternoon, it happens.

"You're on Ashe," I'm told. Mattek's doubles partner, American Angela Haynes, has a second-round singles match. I'm antsy and hoping that Haynes is covered up, and that there are no delays.

When I exit Ashe's tunnel and step on the actual court, I feel as though I'm being swallowed. You look up and humanity is everywhere. *Toto, we're not on Court 18 anymore.* The court seems much, much larger than any of the others, and it has other significant differences. Here, the balls ricochet further off the back fences, the alleys are seemingly endless, and the crowd seems a football field away. At the back of Ashe, balls often disappear into holes behind the court where television camera people are stationed. Inside each of these crevices, a ball person is specifically assigned to retrieve balls. (It's usually assigned to one of the young female ball persons.) Previously, I had declined an opportunity to work this position. It seemed somewhat degrading. My rationale: *You cannot be serious! I'm a ball person. I run after balls!* Now, as I stand on Ashe, I imagine a ball person hunkered down in a cramped space with a camera person just waiting to pounce on a ball so that he or she can toss it back through the thin horizontal opening to the court. I regret not taking this assignment.

On the big stage, I pretend that I'm on the small stage, say Court 18. I block out the crowd and lock in on facilitating the action—and being invisible. Of course, Ashe is very visible with its large crowd, not to mention the television audience. It's the worst place to screw up.

Fortunately, my Ashe debut goes off without a hitch. One of my colleagues, however, isn't so lucky. During the course of a Tommy Haas and Robby Ginepri evening match, a ball rolled into the seating area. At Ashe, fans are allowed to keep balls that go into the stands, just as at baseball games. In this case, I was told that the ball was sitting, unclaimed. One of the older vets, who happened to be balding, retrieved the ball as he should have and returned it to the court. Immediately, this incited the evening crowd. I was told that just about the entire house stood and booed this ball person for not tossing the ball to someone in the crowd. "He's probably giving it to his kid," joked Johnny Mac, who was providing television commentary. This incident was unfortunate on two counts. First, it interrupted the match. Second, it brought to light an open secret: a good number of the ball persons weren't ball boys but ball *men or women*, not the image that Open officials wanted to project, for whatever reason.

—————

After three years of running after balls, my other work gave me no choice but to request an evenings-only schedule. I felt that I'd earned it. After all, I was a former ball person Rookie of the Year runner-up. Unfortunately, the Czar didn't feel the same way, and denied my request. And with that, my Open run was over. Perhaps it was for the best. If the Czar had accepted my terms, I'd probably still be working the courts. Like Nastase, I often don't know when to quit.

—————

A few years after my retirement, I return to the Open to watch an admission-free qualifying match of a player I once shared a court with. Back then, he was a *name* junior. Now, he's just another struggling unknown attempting to make the Main Draw. After I stop by the Perch, where the ball persons are obediently waiting, I see lots of young, hopeful faces. None are familiar. They have no idea that I was one of them, and they ignore me as if I'm invisible.

6

Amateur Caddie

After tennis, it's fitting that I tackle golf.

I volunteer to become an "amateur caddie" at the Travelers Championship, a PGA stop, which is held at the TPC River Highlands course in Cromwell, Connecticut.

On the morning after the U.S. Open golf championship, just after eight, I report to the Volunteer Villa, a large tent, where I sign a waiver and wait. After a while, a large man, the Head Amateur Caddie, addresses us. He's mostly concerned about two things: amateur caddies not being physically able to walk the course with a bag, and soliciting tips. If we do the latter, Head Caddie tells us that we'll be banned from volunteering. Also, he adds that there's no guarantee that we'll be actually walking the course.

Moments later, Head Caddie asks for six bodies.

I'll be walking the course after all.

At the check-in area, right next to the parking lot, I'm in a single-file line, waiting to carry a player's clubs from his car to his cart. (I didn't see any female competitors.) Unfortunately, I won't be caddying for a professional player. The "amateur" in amateur caddie refers to the golfers that we'll be assisting. Eventually, I'm summoned to a black Thunderbird. I deliver Thunderbird's clubs to his assigned cart, where I put on my caddie bib with the player's last name and wait in a procession of golf carts. There, a veteran amateur caddie informs me that there could be some substantial gratuities in today's "volunteer" work. In fact, Veteran Amateur says that he has never been stiffed and was once tipped a $500 gift certificate. I wasn't planning on seeing any cash for today's "volunteering." However, I welcome the idea.

After waiting for about an hour, Head Caddie shows up with a young rookie, who he's concerned about. He places the newbie with the Veteran Amateur and puts me on another cart. Good-bye Thunderbird.

At our final meeting before tee-off, Head Caddie orders us to line up in the order of the hole that we're starting from. My group is starting at tee two, so I'm second in line. As I take my place, Head Caddie hands me a tube of aluminum tinfoil.

Is it a special golf device? I know more about the movie *Caddyshack* than I do about the actual game.

"If you don't like ground beef, let me know," says Head Caddie to everyone. It's a burrito. I don't want to walk on a full stomach—especially a stomach full of burrito. I dig in because, well, it's *there*. As the cart zips along, I swallow it. Actually, there was no need to rush because there's no one at tee two—except myself and a thirteen-year old who's caddying for his father. We have about an hour to kill before our party of four amateurs and one professional is scheduled to arrive. Once again, I wait and try to make small talk with the thirteen-year-old. After that fails miserably, we sit under a tree in silence. I don't want to carry anything—or move, for that matter. It's a beautiful day, and I want another burrito and to drink as much complimentary water as I want.

Eventually, the crew arrives: the other amateur caddies, the official scorer, and the sign carrier, who is referred to in golf circles as the standard bearer, a woman whom no ones seems to acknowledge—except me. I share a connection, albeit unspoken, with the standard bearer. A few months earlier, I had been a standard bearer at the LPGA's Sybase Match Play Championship, which featured sixty-four of the best female players in the world.

=====

For 36 holes, I was basically a human scoreboard. Let's be clear: I didn't keep the official score. I just carried the sign and changed the scoreboard after each hole. Still, it was work. The sign was cumbersome and heavy and each match lasted four-plus hours. Most memorably, for about 5 holes, I carried the sign through a torrential downpour. Fortunately, I wasn't struck by lightning.

I was carrying the sign for the sake of the course spectators, except that there were none. I made the mistake of discussing my standard bearer experience with a colleague. He wasn't impressed.

"You were a sign boy," he blurted at me derisively.

"Actually, I was a standard bearer!" I replied back defensively.

"Sign boy!"

"Standard bearer!" I railed, gritting my teeth. "I was a damn standard bearer!" And I did it with a sense of pride, as if I were leading a fleet of Roman warriors into battle.

———

I ask the official scorer about what to expect from the day, and specifically about the professional golfer that'll be accompanying us. The scorer tells me that he'll be aloof, preparing for tournament play, which is three days away. In other words, the pro will basically be a robot.

As we loiter at tee two, a cart pulls up with a tall, dark-haired, athletic man. In fact, the vehicle has difficulty containing the man's large, gangly frame. He looks like a basketball player. Before the cart comes to a halt, the man enthusiastically leaps off the cart and walks excitedly toward our small entourage. "I got six caddies!" says the man with a warm smile. I haven't a clue who this friendly man is. I'm quite pleased to learn that he's our professional. Just the day before, Michael Putnam finished forty-fifth at the U.S. Open. Michael is one of the elite golfers in the world, but he doesn't act like it. Michael, and his caddie, Putty, introduce themselves, shaking everyone's hands. We're all on a first name basis. Finally, the amateurs show up, and I take the clubs of my golfer. Our amateurs are insurance guys, affiliated with the tournament's sponsors.

At the tee, the eldest member of our crew talks smack. He's chomping on a cigar, boasting that he just endured open heart surgery two months earlier. On the very first hole, my guy hits one well off the fairway, but I don't know where exactly. Unfortunately, my vision isn't the best, and I have no experience in tracking golf balls. I attempt to play the part and scour the weeds. Meanwhile, Michael walks off into the trees—way off the course. I'm not sure that ball went that far awry, but who is this amateur to say anything? Just as I'm about to surrender my search, I find a ball, perhaps even the right ball. "It's here!" I yell excitedly to my guy and Michael, who's far off in the trees. "That's a good caddie!" yells Michael, excited, his back to me as he leans slightly over.

Michael wasn't searching for the ball. He was taking a leak.

With his own caddie, Putty, a slender, bespectacled New Zealander, Michael seems to have an excellent repartee. As they walk, Michael plays reporter, asking Putty what it's like to caddie the U.S. Open. For Putty, it was nothing short of rapturous. As we walk, we're brought back to the previous day. We're walking Bethesda, surrounded by fans whose energy carries us from hole to hole. I need as much inspiration as possible. These clubs aren't light!

At first, I carry my player's clubs with its handle. The bag has straps, but they're somewhat elaborate, and I don't want to ask my guy how to operate them. I always seem to have trouble with straps, whether on shoulder pads or on a golf bag. Fortunately, my guy offers a few strap-related tips, and I place the bag on my back like a backpack, which makes the walk a heck of a lot easier. Not surprisingly, my group of amateurs plays awfully slow. I'm busy carrying the bag and following balls that land far from the center of the fairway. "Blame it on the caddie!" Michael quips when anyone hits a bad shot—and there's a lot of bad shots, so there's lots of blame coming my way. We don't have to worry about just our balls. "Fore!" I hear someone yell faintly, and Open Heart jerks awkwardly. A split second later, a ball lands five yards away from us.

Because of his precarious heart condition, Open Heart has brought along a cart. Often, Open Heart forgets his cart, so he constantly has to walk back to retrieve it. Ultimately, he's doing about as much walking *with* the cart as he would without. Michael is ecstatic that Open Heart has the cart. As frequently as possible, he hitches a ride, standing on the back. Michael must be exhausted. He just played four of the most intense, not to mention successful, rounds of his life. Also, he's traveling the tour with his wife and eight-month-old child, whom he has a picture of on his bag.

After more than two and a half hours of scrambling for and dodging errant balls, we somehow make it to the 10th hole, where there's a mini-buffet of sandwiches, wraps, chips, and soda. At the day's start, Head

Caddie told us to avoid eating unless we're about to faint. I'm not about to collapse, but I'm sweaty, kind of hungry, and it's *there*. Still, I'm hesitant. I'm basically the hired help—except I wasn't hired. I volunteered. But then Michael digs in and encourages everyone to do the same. "Someone's paying for it!" he says. Taking Michael's cue, I grab a banana and half a wrap. What are they gonna do, fire the volunteer? As Michael enjoys some chips and Skittles, he watches the party in front of us get the big-time treatment. An announcer with a mic calls up each amateur and their pro. When the party's pro, Kevin Kisner, a rookie on the tour, is announced, Michael boos him good-naturedly. Next hole, a kid asks Michael for his autograph. Michael gives him his signature, plus some conversation, which is completely one-sided.

Michael listens intently to what the kid has to say.

During the final six holes, the insurance guys start to slack. My guy even gives up on a hole or two. At about the five-hour mark, Michael gets slightly serious for the first time, reminding everyone to keep their focus. Then on 17, Michael tees off with his hat on backward, Billy Madison style. When he gets to the middle of the fairway, he just lies down for a moment. No one cares. No one's around. We're one of the last parties, if not the very last, on the course. On the day's final fairway, one of the insurance guys asks Michael somewhat rhetorically if his job is fun ("Isn't it fun?"). Michael turns serious, explaining that it's work, which can be "fun" at times. Money's at stake, livelihoods, so that's business. With that in mind and the finish line in sight, I start thinking about my tip. Michael is a great guy, but carrying this bag and tracking and dodging these balls is work!

By the final hole (actually hole one), I've gained confidence, and I encourage my guy to stay sharp and finish strong. "Focus!" I command in a low voice. Maybe it helps. During the final stretch, my guy's ball lands twenty-five yards from the green. "Two shots," I command. My guy proceeds to chip one that lands roughly six yards from the hole. As everyone looks on, my guy nails the putt. With the marathon finally over, everyone congratulates one another with handshakes. I award my guy with half a man hug, a lean and a pat on the back. It's awkward because it takes my guy by surprise, and he doesn't wholeheartedly reciprocate.

"It was nice to meet you," Michael tells me as he shakes my hand.

"I'll be rooting for you," I tell him and Putty. I sound like a fan because I am.

I strap my guy's clubs on the back of a cart and climb on the back of another and say farewell, thrilled that we're done—though not a single penny richer. I wasn't tipped for my services. Maybe I should've kept my trap shut on the last hole, or perhaps it was just an oversight. The other amateurs were using friends or relatives as their caddies. Or maybe my guy thought I sucked. Regardless, I'm beat and done with golf for good!

There is one reward, though.

As the insurance guys sort things out on the green, I head back to the clubhouse with the pros. Michael sits shotgun. Putty and I stand on the back.

For the short ride back, I'm one of them.

7

The Real Rollerball

It started with a vision: basketball on in-line skates.

Tom LaGarde, the visionary, wasn't just a 6-foot-10 athletic body. First and foremost, Tom was intelligent and had lots of ideas. Tom also happened to play basketball extremely well. After playing big-time college ball at North Carolina and winning a gold medal in the 1976 Olympics, Tom played in the NBA for several seasons, helping the Seattle Super-Sonics win an NBA championship in 1979.

After retiring from the NBA, Tom didn't play much basketball because of his bad knees, but he was doing a lot of in-line skating. On wheels, his knees felt little or no pain. One day, Tom rolled by a basketball game and had a eureka moment. Soon after, Tom started shooting around—on blades, and he commenced a search for teammates for a new, different brand of basketball. Tom placed an ad in an in-line skating publication, asking for volunteers to join "the world's first-ever roller basketball team."

Just one person answered.

Altitude Lou, a seasoned stunt skater who grew up playing street ball on the Lower East Side with ex-NBAer Jayson Williams, wasn't just any skater. He leaped over taxi cabs on skates and proved to be an ideal sparring partner. In Tompkins Square Park in the East Village, Altitude and Tom waged intense, full-court, one-on-one battles. Eventually, an eclectic mix joined them: the well-employed, the unemployable, the athletic, the unusual—and the just plain weird. There was Al, the subway conductor from Ghana. TK played semi-pro ball in Europe by way of Connecticut. An *almost* playground legend, who called himself Jordan, signed on. And one of the *other* Jordan's former teammates, Bison Dele, formerly

Brian Williams, participated in a few games. Spinner, an industrial artist with a handlebar mustache, arguably the most diehard rollerballer, made sure that the action never hit a lull. "We're burning daylight!" Spinner blared at every opportunity. Tom called this nascent community NIBBL, the National In-line Basketball League, even though it only existed in New York City.

Eventually, Tom came up with roller basketball–specific rules: four-man teams, no inbounding after a conversion, and only one free-throw attempt for two points. As far as traveling, players can roll for five seconds without dribbling. No surprise, traveling can be tough to regulate.

═══

Just as NIBBL is starting to roll, I call Tom for an interview, and we get together for a breakfast meeting. During our discussion, we somehow rotate positions: Tom asks the questions and I tell him about practically growing up on skates and my roller derby aspirations. At the end of breakfast, Tom picks up the tab and I agree to show up at the next roller basketball scrimmage.

Soon enough, I figure out that I can play this new game, for the most part. I can definitely skate. I just don't know how to play basketball. During one highly charged game, my lack of basketball knowledge becomes painfully obvious. As the opposing team was bringing the ball up the court, I yelled time-out. Everyone was ignoring me, so I started yelling louder. I must've come across like one of Will Ferrell's ridiculous characters. Finally, TK cut me off. "You gotta have possession to call time-out!"

As far as shooting, my form was all wrong. Eventually, Tom got tired of my "hoist over the shoulder" slingshot bricks. After a scrimmage, he took me aside and showed me the correct form. During halftime of an exhibition, which we were playing on a hockey rink without lines or refs, so it was basically non-stop action, Tom offered this sage advice: "Rest on offense!" In other words, play D until your heart's gonna burst out of your chest and the offense will follow. We were going at it especially hard that day because maybe a dozen kids with their parents were watching. Hey, they were fans!

I started educating Tom about my Yankee Stadium experience during a road trip to Boston for an exhibition. While Tom had played in sports arenas all over the world, he'd never given much thought to stadium hawking, until I rolled along.

"How do you do it?" Tom asked.

"I just walk around and yell 'Soda,' and fans wave me down or yell out Soda Man to get my attention."

"Soda Man?"

"Yeah, that's what they call me."

Soda Man becomes my nickname, at least in NIBBL.

Eventually, I told Tom about Macarena Night at the stadium, when the entire house did the dance. Tom was into it, really into it. On the spot, right there in the van, we decided to have our very own Macarena Night. For the remainder of the trip, we furiously channel surfed the radio in search of the popular song. When we found it, Tom would blast it and we basically went nuts, singing along at the top of our lungs, with Tom attempting to do the dance from his seat. We didn't know the words—or the moves, for that matter—but we persevered with our version.

It takes a unique man to Macarena with another man.

———

While my basketball knowledge needs work, my NIBBL IQ is high. I embrace all its quirky rules, particularly the one regarding keeping the ball in bounds. In NIBBL, a ball is in play as long as the player with possession has one part of their body, no matter how small, in the court. Just about every NIBBLer ignores this nuance, probably because they're stuck on the rules of conventional basketball. Since I wasn't too familiar with *those* rules, I don't have this problem. Ultimately, I go after balls that are headed out of bounds that everyone ignores. Often, I wind up facedown on the pavement completely extended with one hand on the ball (while a part of one of my skates remains in the court). After this, I call time-out.

Finally, I figured out that rule.

———

After much practice and many, many games, my NIBBL team, the Peace Frogs, is facing a formidable, perhaps unbeatable foe, Puerto Rico, in the semifinals of the NIBBL playoffs. The showdown is scheduled for noon at Union Square, a popular pedestrian hub. My Peace Frogs are the fourth seed, which is no cause for celebration—there are only eight teams in NIBBL.

During the regular season, Puerto Rico had routed us in a humiliating fashion. When the outcome was already decided, Puerto Rico shamelessly ran up the score and showboated à la Los Angeles Lakers circa the Showtime era. They practically started a merengue line! As far as improving roller basketball's visibility, Puerto Rico's antics weren't a bad thing. Hundreds of passersby stopped to watch *their* show at our expense. With roller basketball, this wasn't usually the case. More often than not, spectators stopped for curiosity's sake as if we were an anthropological exhibit.

With their three-headed monster, Puerto Rico was unquestionably the best squad in the talent department. For starters, they had one of NIBBL's founders, crowd-pleaser Altitude Lou, who leaped off ramps to dunk. Altitude was unstoppable in the open court, gliding to the hole seemingly effortlessly, manipulating his body as he hung in the air. During the early years of NIBBL, Altitude was basically the poster boy of the league—that's of course if we had had posters. But that was before his current teammate, Superman, rolled onto the scene and became NIBBL's premier player. A former college player and son of a legendary coach, Superman can do it all, especially shoot. Puerto Rico also had Superman's best friend, Gil, another former college player, who was excellent in his own right. With Superman by his side, Gil's game flourished. Superman and Gil were like yin and yang.

Since the Peace Frogs had been publicly flogged by Puerto Rico, I had developed a repartee with the Peace Frogs' captain, TK, who embraced my game, accentuating my positives. Though I wasn't what you would call a shooter, TK always granted me the green light to shoot, and he worked on my shot with me. We started close to the hole and worked our way back. After each shot, TK passed the rock right back to me. Then, we worked on layups, *just from the left side.*

Prior to this, the only time I went left was in the voting booth.

We shared a common purpose: Puerto Rico payback. We never discussed beating them. We couldn't win a rematch. However, we could show 'em that we belonged on the same court.

> As far as my relationship with TK, there was definitely one un-Miyagi moment. During the NIBBL all-star game, I hit a hanging lefty layup and was feeling it. When TK, who was on the opposing team, got the ball on the very next possession, I rolled in hard, going for the swat. After hitting a big shot, I wanted to get the job done on the other end of the floor, just like the announcers talk about on television. After all, I was an all-star, right? In truth, I was just another player, but I attended every scrimmage and got after it. When I saw TK spotting up, my eyes swelled as I rolled toward him with a full head of steam. I was focused completely on the ball that was about to leave his fingertips. I was gonna reject it and bang my chest. Just as I was about to yell "Get that sh——" we crashed, roller derby style, into the pavement. TK was understandably pretty fired up, and he let me know it. Later, after looking at video of the collision, I was cleared of any intentional wrongdoing. Our wheels had accidentally become entangled.

A week prior to the rematch with Puerto Rico, TK and I connect over the phone. We don't talk about the game, sticking to mundane matters. However, we're letting each other know that we're focused on Puerto Rico. As he speaks, I imagine TK shrouded in beads next to a lava lamp as incense billows. TK's the closest thing NIBBL has to former NBA coach Phil Jackson. Exponentially more than its physical aspects, TK appreciates the mental aspects of the game, which is not surprising, considering his background. His father, TK Senior, whom *Sports Illustrated* named one of the top fifty point guards to come out of New York City, has a firm place in sports history, specifically in the realm of psych-out maneuvers. For the tip-off of the 1957 National Championship basketball game, TK Senior, a 5-foot-11 point guard for the University of North Carolina, was instructed by his coach, Frank McGuire, to take the opening tip against

7-foot-1 Kansas center Wilt Chamberlin. TK Senior lost the tip, but the tone was set, and the Tar Heels went on to win the championship.

TK grew up in the shadow of that play and he was *all* about the mental. TK was no slouch physically, either. The starting point guard on his high school state championship runner-up team, TK had played with a who's who of players, including the Jordans—NIBBL's Jordan and that *other* Jordan. TK was good at making everyone around him better, especially me. I imagine that he could have found a way onto his perennial national contender college team, but for whatever reason, TK didn't aspire to that. TK owned the game. It didn't own him.

Puerto Rico owned us, though. Now, we had a shot at redemption. Winning was not on the menu. Competing was. Just after dawn as the sun started to peek out, some of the most dedicated NIBBLers put aside their team allegiances and met outside a Lower East Side storage area to perform the arduous task of loading the baskets and gear into a van, so it could be taken to Union Square where the baskets were to be erected and the lines were to be sprayed onto the asphalt surface. In a matter of hours, Union Square would be transformed into a basketball arena.

However, not all the players were present. Minutes before the game, we receive confirmation on a rumor: Superman will be arriving after opening tip. No one knows exactly when. Maybe Superman has a real obligation, or perhaps it was a case of hubris: he figures that the Peace Frogs are harmless and will be jettisoned peacefully into oblivion, his presence not required. Now with Superman's attendance in question, our chances of an upset are much, much improved. Even without him, however, Altitude Lou and Gil have more than enough talent to blow us out by themselves. While Superman's absence is a bonus, I'm not overjoyed. TK has me prepared to take on anyone. The Peace Frogs want Puerto Rico's best shot. If we lose, we lose. It's not like we hadn't lost before. If we win, I don't want the asterisk. Before the game, the public address announcer reads off the starting lineups over the loudspeakers. This first-rate treatment, courtesy of Tom's outstanding preparation, is appreciated but completely unnecessary. We're the early show on Saturday. Besides the actual participants and Tom, *no one's* at the game, *not even one aspiring anthropologist!*

Just before tip-off, TK gathers us. He places one hand in the middle and then the other. Everyone follows his lead. TK isn't acting like himself—or Phil Jackson, for that matter. He's acting like he did when I tackled him unintentionally. I swear, unintentionally! He intensely barks this out:

No plays off!

Rebound hard!

We own every loose ball!

Leave it all out on the court!

Let's go!

Peace Frogs!

Per TK's orders, I'm raring to go. I'm prepared to hit the deck for any and every loose ball. In fact, I'll hit the deck and keep going. I'll dig into that asphalt and keep digging. I'll work on the city's water main. I'll be a sandhog!

In truth, I might as well have been underground. Perhaps there's something to be said for being too psyched. It doesn't matter. Little Country, our de facto point guard, has come to play. (Around this time, a popular player at Oklahoma State was nicknamed Big Country.) A former college hockey player, able to pivot on skates like a gamer's joystick, Little Country pushes the ball up the court in a hurry, before hitting an array of shots from, well, everywhere. Little Country might not be the best roller basketball player, but he's the league's best overall athlete. Little Country could rally with Roger in the morning, play a loop with Tiger in the afternoon, and run a marathon or two after all that. With Little Country lighting it up, each Peace Frog's role is clear. Little Country is what you would call a scorer because he's always looking to get the ball in the hole. TK is a passer, always looking for the open guy, setting people up. Andre is a hybrid because he shoots and passes. As for myself, I'm neither a shooter nor a passer. I'm the guy who makes the pass *before* the pass.

Tom keeps stats on every imaginable category, except one: THE PASS BEFORE THE PASS!

In the first few minutes after tip-off, it's painfully obvious that Puerto Rico has taken us lightly, and they don't care much for defense, which they usually have no need for. Always, almost immediately after the opening tip, they knock teams into submission with their multitude of offensive weapons. Also, there's the spectator factor: no one is at the game, not even a few confused tourists, which works to our advantage. Altitude Lou lives for playing in front of a crowd. As a crowd-pleasing gesture, Altitude had even dyed his hair green, which was somewhat inexplicable because we play with helmets on. With no crowd, Altitude is just plain Louie, still awesome but a mere human.

In the early minutes, we're ahead double digits. Puerto Rico picks up the intensity and attempts to counterpunch, but without Superman they're out of sync. We're not helping by getting back on defense, not allowing Altitude to get into the open court, where he's deadly. We've forced Puerto Rico into a half-court, methodical game. With Little Country demanding the ball, I reiterate to myself Tom's advice imparted at that exhibition: "Rest on offense!" My goal is to stay between Altitude and the hole and stop the ball. As I shadow Altitude, my back to the basket, Altitude jerks, jives, starts, and stops, all in an effort to shake me. Altitude goes left, I go left. Altitude goes right. I go right. I don't watch his head or eyes. Instead, I stay glued to his hips. TK says to always watch the hips. Often, my face-off with Altitude reaches this crescendo: a low-percentage outside shot with my hand in Altitude's face. In another matchup, Gil and TK are having their own private tango in the paint. With his broad shoulders, Gil aggressively charges to the hole, and finds that he has absolutely nowhere to go. TK refuses to fall for any of Gil's head fakes because he's watching his hips.

After all this hip watching, TK and I should take up ballroom dancing.

Without Superman, Gil is a ying minus a yang, and Altitude is stuck in the runway. It's almost too easy. I even scored. When no one was within a two-mile radius of me, I hit my lay-ups! At the half, Peace Frogs are up by 30 and change.

No lead is safe in roller basketball. Still, there hasn't been a Superman sighting and Puerto Rico is deflated, bickering among themselves. Even though the game is far from over, we behave as if it is, lapsing into a place of complacency as we rehydrate. We're confident that we'll be playing for the championship tomorrow, something we didn't dare fathom an hour earlier. TK is relaxed, talking to a few of his friends. If we had champagne, we'd crack it open.

Minutes into the second half, a wrench is flung into our championship aspirations. Superman shows, and he hits the court with a vengeance, playing with our first-half urgency and then some. We guard him but not too aggressively because we don't want to foul, stop the clock, and give up easy points from the free-throw line. We want this game over *yesterday*. It doesn't matter. Not warmed up and hurried, Superman is missing. With Superman ice cold, we actually extend our lead while not playing particularly well.

Eventually, Superman finds his stroke. Even if he tried, he can't miss, hitting an array of circus shots, including some way-out, four-point shots (another NIBBL innovation). We close on Superman, but he just backs up and keeps stroking, nothing but net. Think Reggie Miller versus the Knicks. Superman's energy ignites his teammates. With Superman back and a burgeoning crowd on hand, Louie transforms back to Altitude Lou and Gil thrives, putting back any of Superman's misses. Superman and Gil—they're back to yinging and yanging. And then they start to talk trash. No one would confuse either of them with Kevin Garnett, but they're damn annoying. After finding their offense, Puerto Rico picks up their defensive intensity and there seems to be a lid on the basket for us. A once certain Peace Frog victory is now in jeopardy, and we have no one to blame but ourselves. With the big lead we got complacent and we did the unpardonable: we stood around on offense.

With just minutes remaining, we still have the lead—by a shoe string. Puerto Rico has cut it to single digits and has all the momentum. Now, Altitude is at the line—at least I think it was Altitude. The action is intense, and I'm a bit delirious. Puerto Rico needs the easy points or at least a rebound so they can kick the ball out to Superman for a four-pointer. Under any circumstances, we cannot allow that. As I wait at the line, TK rolls past me and whispers three words to me: "Get the ball!" Easier said than done. I lock in. As I wait at the line, I repeat the free-throw rule to myself: wait for the ball to leave Altitude's hands . . . With a nice crowd now framing the sidelines, Altitude steps to the line. In any other circumstance, I'd be rooting for Altitude. He's a soft-spoken showman, not to mention a fellow pioneer. I won't forget his spectacular three-pointer from the top of the key during halftime of a Nets game at the Meadowlands, arguably the sweetest shot in NIBBL history. Today, however, I'm rooting for Altitude to brick it. As Altitude eyes the rim, he bounces the ball once . . . twice . . . three times . . . When Altitude finally releases, I jut out like a rodeo bull. As the ball clanks the rim, bodies collide. It's a roller derby in the crease. The refs swallow their whistles. When the dust clears, I'm on my knees near the sideline with the ball. "Time-out!"

My two specialties: loose balls and calling time-out.

Now, we attempt to run the clock, playing not to lose, as we had done for much of the second half. Unfortunately, we turn it over, and Puerto Rico winds up right back at the line. I can't tell you exactly who because I'm locked in on one thing, getting the ball. I don't have to be told twice.

Again, bodies collide and there's a pileup, or at least it feels like one. Somehow, I come up with the ball again. I'm locked in. Perhaps it's because I feel like I owe it to TK. TK never told me *not* to shoot, and he made me a starter.

Then again, he didn't have much of a choice. We only have four players on our four-man squad.

After my second rebound, Puerto Rico can't rebound. Ultimately, they run out of time. As the final seconds wind down, Little Country plays keep away, dribbling out the clock. Puerto Rico, NIBBL's Goliath, has been vanquished. I raise my arms in the air. Relief! Following the 1983 NCAA national championship basketball game, when his team upset a heavily favored Houston team, North Carolina State coach Jim Valvano wandered the court searching for someone, anyone, to embrace. I don't have Valvano's concern. I lose myself in the moment. At half court, I roll directly into TK's arms. We embrace, wholeheartedly—and I *mean* wholeheartedly—both arms, full body. No awkward man hug here. It's our *From Here to Eternity* moment. For all I know, NIBBL reserved us a room. The rest of the Peace Frogs join in, I think, but I can't be quite sure. I'm oblivious to everything. If any anthropologists were in the crowd, they probably would have said, "These basketball guys on skates are really emotional."

Then, I wake up.

We upset Puerto Rico. But now it's Sunday morning and there's another game to play against Tom's team. In a way, I don't want to play another game. I want to walk away from the table ahead. I'm still euphoric from Puerto Rico.

In the championship game, I don't even know if I scored or made an assist. It doesn't matter. The Peace Frogs are on a roll, and we're clearly better than Tom's team, at least on that day. In the second half with us firmly in lead, I find myself in the paint with Tom. It's roller derby time again, and we're scrapping.

> During one scrimmage, Tom got in my grill when he deemed my play too aggressive with NBAer Bison Dele, who at 6-foot-11, two hundred and sixty pounds, was way bigger than I was, to say the least. (I swear I was in control and did not push Dele around!) In retrospect, I can live with the fact that I went toe to toe with Dele, who won a world championship with the Chicago Bulls.

I wind up facedown on the pavement and have to exit the game. After wrapping a good portion of my head in gauze, I return. I'm not doing anything productive because I can't really see. I'm a bad Halloween costume.

Afterward, I need a couple of stitches. It's not the first time. I don't lead the leagues in scoring, assists, rebounds, or even passes before the pass, if that category existed.

I lead the league in stitches.

I never planned it that way. I was always going for the ball. There was the time that Uwe's (NIBBL's import "from Sweden," according to our announcer) elbow found my face when I was going for a rebound. Another time, attempting a steal, my face found Tom's elbow. I could go on and on.

As I'm waiting in the emergency room waiting area, I'm finally coming down, recalling the day. Sure, I'm pleased that we won the championship, but my showdown with Tom in the paint overshadows all this. You see, Tom has played and outplayed the best of the best: Larry, Magic, the Ice Man, to name just a few. While Tom is always awesome, no one expects much from me. If I hit a shot, everyone gets a snow day! Tom gave me his best shot, nothing less. I came out on the short end. But how shall I put it?

I'm worthy.

HALFTIME

Go ahead. Get up and use the facilities and then grab a snack. There probably isn't a line for either. Get some tap water too. It's free! When you return, I don't have a band or a halftime show for you. I've got something better: a pep talk.

———

First, congrats on making it this far. Give yourself a hand. It's not easy being a reader these days. It probably would've been easier to Twitter away your time. But you're old school and you're tough and focused. Now, you're in the home stretch, and I implore you to finish. Do not quit on me or yourself! Close this out and get to the final word. Then, immediately, go Twitter about it!

8

Back to the Majors

I was sucking more than A-Rod in the playoffs. I wasn't writing, and I needed a spark. The ballpark had inspired me once before, so I returned. On a frigid March day, I show up at my Field of Dreams, Shea Stadium, where I wait in line outside for several hours. Inside, I wait in yet another line in a non-descript stadium hallway. Then, there's a written test. It's elementary: addition, subtraction, and common sense.

Somehow, I make it to the next round.

Weeks later, I sit with a few dozen other hopefuls in a room at the stadium as a polished middle-aged man addresses us. With his solid, sturdy frame and shiny coif and matching mustache, he looks very professional. He could be a banker. As far as vending, this man is the General Manager, the General for short. The General makes all vending decisions—who sells what and where—and he speaks of concessions sales as if it's a noble endeavor. Fans work hard all week, the General believes, and they deserve the option of having a concessions item delivered directly to their seat, promptly and professionally. In a way, the General, a former vendor, is serving a slice of the American dream. Later, I learned that the General's father held the position he holds now. It's a family business.

Now, the General is inviting us into his inner sanctum, offering us an opportunity. If we're to accept, we're to act as professionals. Since we're paid, we're no longer amateurs, the General explains. We're to be punctual, polite, and loud—very loud. With glee, the General recalls hearing a vendor calling out their item while he watched the game at home on television. In closing, the General gives us two rules that we must obey, no exceptions:

Do not lie.

Do not steal.

If we commit either, the General makes it clear in no uncertain terms that we face banishment and possibly imprisonment.

———

It feels nothing like early April. It's sunny, but the temperature is barely out of the thirties. For Opening Day, I'm running late. As usual, the 7 train is crawling. We're scheduled to report three hours before first pitch, which seems a bit excessive to me. After all, we're not hourly employees. We're on straight commission, 13 percent in my case.

When I finally report about twenty minutes late, the General says nothing. As he points to his watch, he simply raises an eyebrow. The General can do calisthenics with his brows. After I apologize profusely, he orders me to fill out a vendor card (with my name and social security digits) and enter the catastrophe that is Shea. A circular, seemingly senseless labyrinth of ramps that appears to be near collapse, Shea is certainly no Fenway or Wrigley in the charm department.

In a barely functioning, tight men's room, I put on my official uniform: a fluorescent yellow T-shirt with the word "vendor" in black capital letters on the back. With my black pants and black shoes, I look like a bumblebee. I have a few hours before first pitch, plenty of time to ponder my assignment. My tardiness could earn me something brutal. Perhaps the General will assign me to the Cheap Seats, where the aisles are exhaustingly long and steep, to sell sunflowers seeds, though such an item isn't on the Shea concessions menu. For slackers in need of a wake-up call, the General will make an exception, or so he'd often like to quip in his unmistakable, wry way.

Instead I'm assigned its distant cousin: popcorn in the field-level seats. I'm apprehensive about popcorn. When I hawked it at Madison Square Garden, the hockey fans smelled blood and told me to get lost, except in much fouler language. I report to the Pit, where the popcorn is *supposed* to be made. After waiting around an hour or so, someone finally produces the popcorn and the vendors scoop and package it into rectangular cardboard containers. I'm a popcorn vendor *not* a popcorn packager. I could complain, but who would listen? I'm a first-day, slightly tardy popcorn hawker. With three or four other harried popcorn vendors scooping from the same batch, every kernel is a tussle. When I'm done filling my first load of twenty boxes, I hand a chip to the checker, an overseer who monitors how much vendors are selling. Now the hard part: selling. Popcorn isn't cheap, so I expect a battle, and it's already the third inning. As far as the vending, our game is nearly half over. At Shea, vendor quitting time is the top of the eighth.

After more than four hours of waiting and loitering, the sun hits me in the eyes as I come out of the tunnel and into the stands.

I'm back in the Majors.

I probably should have never left. I missed almost everything about it, including the flexible hours and the paycheck. In the stands, I ignore the game on the field. I'm back to playing my private game. I've got time to make up, so I work fast. Surprisingly, sales are strong. Here's a news flash: people come to the ballpark for the game and to stuff their faces, and not necessarily in that order. Lots of kids are playing parentally consented hooky, and in no time I'm back in the Pit dueling for kernels. By the eighth, about sixty boxes later, I go to the Money Room, where I wait to return my remaining chips, as well as the cash I owe the house, which I hand to a man behind a glass wall. After my take goes through a cash counter, the man gives me the thumbs up, signaling that I've handed in the correct amount. With tips I made about $100, not bad for a slightly tardy vendor making a comeback. About eight hours after I've begun, I'm ready to crawl back to the train.

———

After the chaotic first day, I'm not late again. For a regular game, vendors have to report just two hours before first pitch. As directed, I show up at Shea's employee entrance and get in formation, which consists of two parallel lines. Union vendors (veterans) and non-union vendors (mostly rookies) form separate lines. Like clockwork, without introduction, the General exits the stadium and conducts an informal inspection. As he methodically works his way through each line, he gives each of us the once-over, raising a brow at such eyesores as five o'clock shadow and soiled uniforms. In the case of Hackett, who actually speaks somewhat like the late stand-up Buddy Hackett, the General has probably given up hope. No matter the day, Hackett is disheveled; his trousers sometimes sag so that his butt is visible, and he always seems to be rambling loudly in his nasal whine. The General is tough, but Hackett has been around seemingly forever, and the General appears to be aware that Hackett is an eternal eccentric, to put it mildly, so he gives him a pass. The General has some Father Flanagan in him.

In the vending force, there's no shortage of eccentrics. There's the Goth, who sometimes dresses in black and on occasion wears a trench coat and platform shoes. As he vends, Headphones listens to headphones. The Mummy walks the stands as if he's among the walking dead and calls out his item in an emotionless monotone. Sergeant Pepper has a tattoo of one of the Beatles and is somewhat of a mystery, prone to standing still and just staring off during the course of a game. No matter how unusual we might be, the General wants us to look reasonably well groomed. When he is done with his inspection, he simply nods, and we're allowed to enter Shea. Now, there's more than an hour and a half to kill. When you're a rookie, nobody really talks to you. Actually, vendors as a whole aren't the most verbal bunch. However, there are two brothers, Heckle and Jeckle, who look almost identical, and they have *a lot* to say. Invariably, they want to get involved in any and every conversation, invited or otherwise. In all of sports, there might not be a more annoying set of brothers—well, maybe Duke's Plumlees. The majority of vendors think of vending as a sideline, something to supplement their main jobs. Vendors teach, deliver mail, drive trains—whatever it takes. Heckle and Jeckle are vendors and that's it. While the job lasts only a few hours, Heckle and Jeckle seem to live it 24/7, and they consider themselves to be the best in the business. "Everyone knows us," I hear one of them boast on multiple occasions. When he says *everyone*, he means everyone remotely involved with vending *in the country, perhaps the world.* But Heckle and Jeckle aren't only obsessed with their numbers—how much they're selling—but what other vendors are making (or not making). And they're cutthroat about it. In vendor speak, cutthroat means that you'll do just about anything for a sale, including screwing another vendor. If you're selling more than Heckle and Jeckle, you'll more than likely find a spot on their shit list. I find them interesting and one of them seems somewhat affable, at least in small doses. However, I quickly learn that his brother has an awful mean streak, prone to unprovoked, malicious comments. Unfortunately, I can't tell them apart. To play it safe, I attempt to stay clear of both. Most vendors do the same. However, sometimes Heckle and Jeckle are unavoidable.

Firsthand, I witness them incite an elite hot dog vendor, Houdini, whose hands work with the speed and precision of a master illusionist when preparing a dog. In record time—that is, of course, if there was a record—Houdini is able to pluck a roll out of the aluminum bin with a fork and place it in a wrapper, then stab a dog with that same fork and place it in that very bun and wrap it, all without the use of his bare hands, which is strictly forbidden. Houdini has off-the-charts sales numbers, and he has a conspicuous spot on Heckle and Jeckle's shit list. Somehow it has gotten back to Heckle and Jeckle that Houdini is allegedly using his bare hands to expedite sales. After one game, Heckle and Jeckle wait until no one is around in the Pit and ambush him, going right for the jugular. "Try and do it without using your hands!" one of the brothers yells at Houdini—at least that's what I think he said. It's a quick hit. As Heckle and Jeckle have intended, Houdini is enraged. I think that Houdini may actually pick up his long, sharp fork and attack them. Before Houdini can act, though, Heckle and Jeckle are out the Pit's door, gone. It's a typical Heckle and Jeckle hit-and-run job.

I never sell popcorn again. Instead, the General puts me on soda— plastic bottles of cola, regular and diet, in the upper mezzanine. Soda can be a bitch. It's heavy, expensive, and not a big seller during the chilly first days of spring. Also, customers are less compelled to tip on it. With soda, for whatever reason, customers seem to be more aware that they're being overcharged. Also, they're not allowed to keep the cap because management believes that bottles with caps have the potential to become weapons. Inevitably, capless sodas lead to conflict between customer and vendor. Almost without exception, customers insist that I leave the cap on the bottle. Prepared for such resistance, I quickly explain the stadium's capless policy. More often than not, the customers begrudgingly back off, accepting the capless soda as just another indignity of attending a professional sporting event. They've already been charged hefty fees for tickets and parking. Capless soda just completes the package. However, there are a few customers who are truly outraged and don't back down, demanding a refund and giving me a *take that* look. Good for them but bad for me, because my soda load isn't getting lighter. Since the trays are quite heavy, vendors place them atop their heads. For me, this practice is somewhat painful. Later, I learn that vendors remove the metal clip at the top of their caps to make this practice bearable. Many vendors also place napkins inside their caps to provide cushion and absorb perspiration. Though it seems quite logical, I never use the napkin technique.

There are a few regular soda vendors, guys who hawk soda game in, game out. The regular soda guys work downstairs on the Field, where the stairs are easy and fans tend to be more generous. There's another regular soda seller, who's more conspicuous. She's one of only a few female vendors. (Of the female vending force, two are longtime veterans and the small handful of others are just rank and file, meaning they don't sell the holy grail of concessions: beer.) Unlike the other female vendors, Soda Woman makes no effort whatsoever to hide her femininity. Her shirt is usually stretched tight over her chest, and she often wears tight, form-fitting black slacks. If you can't see her, you're certain to hear her. She has an unmistakable pitch, more like an abbreviated song. "Hey Sodah!" Soda Woman chirps, usually smiling. "Hey Sodah!" Even with the soda atop her head, Soda Woman seems to slightly sway her hips, which can't hurt as far as tips. I know of at least one fan that brought her a souvenir from his vacation. When I sell soda in her section, customers specifically request her. "Where's the girl?" one guy asks me. It is a frustrating, slow night, and I ignore him, continuing to walk down the steps. Then, I stop, unable to help myself. "You want the girl?" I ask. The guy looks up, surprised. He doesn't say anything. When I actually attempt to engage fans in conversation, that's often the response I get. Often, it seems as though fans take vendors for mindless robots, and don't know how to respond when we actually speak. We're way up in the Cheap Seats, far, far away from the General. No chance that he can spot me and assign me sunflower seeds.

"You want the girl?" I repeat.

"Yeah," the guy finally responds.

"Hey Sodah!" I chirp in my best Soda Woman voice, even swaying my hips a little. I have to do the latter. If I am gonna do Soda Woman, I have to go all the way.

I don't get the sale—not even close.

I don't mind hearing Soda Woman's sing-song sales delivery, but I don't love working with her because she's cutthroat, too, just not as overt as Heckle and Jeckle. When we share the same section, the Cheap Seats, she spots me working my way around the stadium, methodically going from aisle to aisle. Instead of hitting a completely different section, Soda Woman enters my next aisle. Before I can say anything, it's over: Soda Woman has hijacked my aisle, forcing me elsewhere.

———

As the season progresses, I can't help but notice the brisk sales of cotton candy, especially on weekends, when the stadium is packed with kids. Though he could sell any item he so desires, including the holy grail, the stadium's most well-known vendor, Superstar, a retired firefighter who travels cross-country (by plane) to work home stands, hawks cotton candy. After games near the Money Room, Superstar looks like one ecstatic retiree. When vendors land a good-selling item, they often want to keep it on the down low because they don't want rival vendors requesting it and potentially snatching their lucrative spot. Superstar's putting up such stellar numbers that he can't hide his success. No one can challenge him, though. Superstar has seniority, and he appears to be in excellent standing with the General. Looking to sample his success, I request cotton candy on my vendor card.

As far as fulfilling requests, the General offers no guarantees. Sometimes, a request can backfire. A vendor might ask for dogs on the Field, and the General might accommodate halfway, assigning dogs in the Cheap Seats. These two assignments are night and day. In the Cheap Seats, tips will be lighter and your legs will feel much, much heavier from the steep incline. This day, the General grants my request: cotton candy in the upper mezzanine. I'm no stranger to the item, having sold it at Madison Square Garden during Christmas shows. However, this is an entirely new ball game. Now I'm dealing with the elements, and it's windy, which I hadn't factored into the equation. I figure that I can deal. As I pick up my wooden board, which has fifty blue cotton candy bushels on it, I'm confident. Moments after I get to the seats, an unexpected gust of wind blows a few bushels out of my board and onto the ground. Immediately, I give chase. Fortunately, the bushels are wrapped in plastic and, also fortunately, I track them down in a moment or two. Relieved and somewhat embarrassed, I retreat to the entrance tunnel, safe from the wind—or so I think. Just as I enter, another gust gets hold of the wad of bills that I'm clutching. Bills fly, the wind pinning them to the walls of the tunnel. I abandon ship, actually my board, leaving it on the floor as I scramble for the bills. After I manage to recover the cash, one of the General's aides chides me for putting my board on the ground and gives me an impromptu seminar on cotton candy hawking.

First rule: confirm that every hole on the board is occupied. (Sometimes the cotton candy preparers leave out a hole or two, leaving the seller short.) Next, go under the board and bend the sticks around the board, so the bushels can't escape no matter how windy it is. Last, when you hit the stands, proceed as if you're a wind sailor. Similar to a sail, the board should be slanted and the bushels should face the wind.

There was another veteran cotton candy vendor in my section who could've provided these very same pointers, but he didn't, because he wanted me to fail miserably, so he could increase his sales numbers.

He's cutthroat, too.

After the seminar and selling a few trays, just as I'm starting to get the hang of it, I'm told that there's no more cotton candy. It's tough to make, and you can't save it for the next day. Before quitting time, cotton candy often runs out. The Genius, a vendor who comes up with conspiracy theories faster than he's able to articulate them, uses cotton candy as an arbiter of whether a game will be played when rain is in the forecast. According to the Genius, if cotton candy is produced, the teams will find a way to get the game in. Conversely, if cotton candy is not made, no baseball will be played. With no cotton candy for me to sell and still feeling a bit wounded from my earlier embarrassing episode, I want to depart, but it's not going to happen. It's only the fifth, and the General doesn't send vendors home early or tolerate laziness. During one of his more memorable pre-game State of the Unions, during which he stands atop a cafeteria bench, and we look up at him as if he's, well, the Almighty, the General told us he was outraged that some vendors had allegedly stopped hawking during the sixth. Then, the General vowed that he would carefully watch the stadium's security video footage and weed out the slackers. Ultimately, the General finds me some soda, and I sell to the bitter, bitter end.

Some of my favorite games turn out to be weekday matinees. Technically, I'm working, but I feel as if I'm playing hooky. Mostly, these weekday affairs have the potential to be good because vendor attendance is usually light, and the stadium is teeming with kids, which isn't necessarily good. At the ballpark, all kids are not equal. If it's an early-season game, there'll be schoolkids. (I have no idea why it's sanctioned that they spend a school day at the ballpark.) In the summer, it's camp kids. Camp kids tend to have deep pockets. If it's hot, and you've got a cool item such as ice cream or ices on one of these camp days, you can count on a big haul, about $150. However, there's a price to pay as far as dealing with kids. Not surprisingly, kids don't tip, and they're almost always annoying. "How much?" they ask incessantly, ignoring the price badge that's pinned to my chest. Of course, they have no intention of making a purchase.

During one weekday matinee, I decide to get a little payback against some annoying camp kids who repeatedly inquire about the price. Instead of continuing to respond, I ignore them completely, walking straight past them without even turning. Perhaps it isn't the most mature thing, but it's humid, pretzel sales are hellacious—and, well, the kids had it coming. When I get to the top of the aisle, though, someone is yelling at me. It's their counselor, who is aggressively charging toward me.

"You should tell them the price!" he yells angrily.

At this point, I probably should've walked away, but I think that might acknowledge some guilt on my end, so I charge back at him, which is akin to taking my gloves off during a hockey game.

"I told them the price!" I bark back.

Before I can get to him, the counselor has second thoughts and sits down, fortunately for both of us.

"No you didn't," he yells from his seat.

"Keep control of your kids. I'll worry about the vending!"

Then I address the kids directly.

"Does anyone want a pretzel?" I ask.

As expected, there is no response. I ask again. The kids don't say a word, nor does their counselor.

A moment later, I walk to another aisle. A veteran vendor is going at it verbally with an usher. I gather that they had bumped into each other accidentally. (Sometimes, ushers camp out in front of an aisle, blocking fans from walking to their seats while a batter is at the plate.) Just when the dispute seems to be over, my colleague starts walking back toward the usher for more. He is annoyed and his vendor muscles are working. I think that nothing good will come of it, so I intervene.

"It's over," I tell him, stepping in front of him, directing him to the adjacent aisle. He walks away. Later, he thanked me.

In moments, I have transformed myself from Dirty Harry to the King Solomon of concessions.

I have perhaps my most unfortunate kid encounter before a Paul Mc-Cartney concert. In the corridor, where I've camped out with my dog bin, a kid runs over to me out of breath. In his excitement, a small drop of saliva flies out of his mouth, hitting me squarely in the face.

"Do you know where pizza is?" he asks, ignoring his saliva deposit on my cheek.

"Are you aware that you just spit on me?" I snarl.

"Sorry."

Wiping my face in disgust, I point to a random food stand, where there is a mob of people and hopefully *no* pizza.

———

During one mid-day matinee, I feel like I've hit the jackpot because it's a scorcher, and I've got ices in the upper mezzanine, which is crammed with wealthy camp kids. In an instant, though, my happiness disappears. Heckle or Jeckle, I'm not sure which, is in my section, selling ices as well. Before the game, Jeckle and I pack our pouches in silence without incident. It's all very civilized. Before we depart for the seats, Jeckle turns to me and throws down the gauntlet. "If you don't do fourteen boxes, you suck!" he barks. Before I can respond, Jeckle is gone. Typical Heckle and Jeckle hit-and-run. Before the challenge, I was planning a nice carefree, lucrative day at the ballpark. Now, it's war. I devise a game plan: Work the visual. Cover space. Stand in front of an aisle, show the bag with the name of the item, be loud, and get waved down. Make the transaction and do it all over again. Unfortunately, Jeckle has done what he intended: he's gotten inside my head. For the rest of the game, I hear Jeckle: *If you don't do fourteen boxes, you suck!* Yes, I'm competing against Jeckle, and he's selling as if he's engaged in a holy war. It's not about the money today. It's not about the action on the field. It's about *our* game in the stands. I sell hard, as if my life depends on it. I'm also playing a cat-and-mouse game with Jeckle, attempting to stay clear of him, hoping that he'll waste time and energy on aisles I've already worked.

I'm cutthroat!

We battle until not a single ice remains. Ultimately, it's close, very close. If it were a boxing match, it would be a split decision. If I lose, there will be no regrets. I left it all out in the stands.

I sold thirteen boxes.

———

If a vendor dislikes the assignment, he or she doesn't have much recourse. With a hundred vendors or so to manage a game, the General can't and won't listen to complaints regarding assignments. We'll sell what we get—and that's it. It's no democracy. Eventually, I settle into a regular item: pretzels, usually in the Cheap Seats. Pretzels are a rookie item because they're carried in a heavy metal canister, which holds a Sterno flame at its bottom, so it can't really be held atop your head (like soda) unless you don't mind your head feeling as if it's on fire. Unlike dogs, pretzels are not an obligatory ballpark buy. Whether they like dogs or not, many fans almost feel compelled to have a dog at the stadium. Pretzels don't have that same cache.

However, I soon learn that pretzels can become quite enticing, especially after a few beers, and they cost $4.25, which is either a bad or a beautiful scenario. When a customer makes the $4.25 payment, you have to study their fingers. If they're pressing down, they're holding a quarter, and you have to be careful that the coin doesn't get dropped under the seats. Approximately a third of pretzel purchasers hand you a $5 and tell you to keep the change, even in the Cheap Seats. Some people are just generous—or maybe they're just bombed. When a customer buys a single pretzel and hands me a ten- or a twenty-dollar bill, I'm careful making change. I hold out the bills like an accordion, so I can view each one. After handing back the bills, I deliver the seventy-five cents separately, so there's less of a chance that the coinage will find the pavement.

Often, when I'm conducting the mini-excavation in my smock for the coinage, customers have an epiphany and tell me to keep the change. That is a beautiful thing. Vendors refer to gratuities as "subway," which has an alternative meaning. When vendors tip Pit workers, that's also often referred to as subway. At orientation, the General strictly forbade vendors from tipping coworkers. He believes that this practice could potentially lead to or actually be bribery for "free" product. Despite the General's stern warning, vendors almost always tip Pit workers, who expect and often demand it. If vendors don't tip these workers, slow and angry service may be suffered as a consequence.

Besides the fact that it's not an obligatory buy, pretzels can be problematic. The Pit always seems to run out, and they're difficult to make. Before I get them in my canister, the pretzels have to be defrosted, topped with salt, and heated in an enormous, Sterno-heated furnace that looks as if it were salvaged from the Stone Age. Perhaps the toughest part of the pretzel preparation is removing them from this furnace, which is quite narrow and extremely hot. Unfortunately, the Pretzel Preparer, a very tall, thin man who wears his pants well beneath his waist, doesn't have the proper utensil for pretzel removal, so he's often forced to use his hands (sometimes bare), making every removal somewhat painful. When a load is finally ready, I hand in my chip to the Pit's checker, Scorecard. For each load that goes out to the stands, Scorecard marks an X next to the appropriate vendor's name on a sheet. He puts an inordinate amount of care into making sure that the X is as perfectly straight as possible. His Xs deserve a standing O! There are lots of Xs to be drawn because every item that's on the stadium's vending menu comes out of this particular pit.

This pit is home to some unique vendors. The Professor, a longtime veteran, stands out. "Ice-cold Beer!" the former college professor hawks in his distinct, deep voice. Even through the white noise of the stadium, it's tough to not hear the Professor, one of the the General's favorites.

During his pre-game State of the Unions, the General mentions the Professor's professionalism, lauding him for walking up every step of every aisle. At the end of an evening, I often see the General and the Professor conversing, enjoying a post-game smoke in the quarantined smoking area just outside Shea.

In Scorecard's Pit, there are a few regular dog vendors. When Zeus raises his dog bin high above his broad shoulders, he's reminiscent of a Greek god. Like many of the vendors, he's worked at the stadium for years. Years ago, Zeus was a ball player, good enough to earn a scholarship. Instead of taking it, Zeus opted to work at the ballpark. Years later, his athleticism is still apparent. He has soft hands, which is beneficial for quickly opening buns on the fly and stabbing dogs. Zeus doesn't regret not taking the scholarship, to say the least. "Vending is the best job in the world," he tells me one day before a game as he chows down a pre-game meal. We are sitting in the lower mezzanine of an empty Shea watching the sprinkler system water the sun-drenched diamond. At that precise moment, it does indeed seem like the best job in the world.

Then, there's Lifer, a slender man. Everyone expects Lifer to never leave stadium work. Even when he's not working, Lifer shows up at the stadium—but not necessarily for the game. Lifer enjoys having a few beers and watching his fellow colleagues sweat. He's proud to be a vendor and enjoys whatever camaraderie there is—and there's not much. We're independent contractors, basically pitted against one another for sales. Lifer, however, wants to be part of a unified vendor tribe. Despite his efforts, Lifer feels somewhat insecure among vendors, at least sometimes. At one point, I overhear Lifer saying that he feels left out because he's white and most of the dog vendors in his section are black. At the stadium, race is a non-issue. I attribute this in large part to the General's leadership. "Treat everyone the way you would want to be treated," the General often tells us. And that covers that.

As far as vendors not keeping a commitment, the General says this: "As far as excuses, death, your own, is acceptable. After that, not much." Even when the General is disciplining us, which is *all* the time, he makes most of us smile. He's also inspirational.

At least in part, the General inspires me to finally sit down and write this. No excuses. Get it down on the page!

Before first pitch, the General usually gives a pep talk, his pre-game State of the Union. During the game, as I work the stairs and hawk, my experiences incubate in my mind. Away from the ballpark, whenever I have the chance, I sit down and stare at the blank page, which is my nemesis. Smoking Joe had Ali. Agassi had Sampras. I have the blank page, which can be intimidating. It's so easy to walk away from the blank page and procrastinate. But I don't want to be just another guy in the playground talking about how I could've been a contender. Players have to do it on the field. I have to do it on the page. I've done the adventure. Now, I have to write about it. It's a package deal. So I bear up and stare down the blank page. I stare hard. Finally, if I'm lucky, ever so tentatively, I begin to type away.

=====

I come up with a pitch to take my mind off the physical grind of selling pretzels in the Cheap Seats. "Hot! Hot! Hot!" I call out. It's not just the words. It's how I say them, somewhat like a crazed kung fu fighter. Immediately, it gets attention and just maybe a few sales. "Hot! Hot! Hot!" some fans yell right back at me. When Lifer hears it, he smiles and yells it back at me. At first, I think that Lifer is giving me a hard time. Soon, I figure out that Lifer is paying me tribute by imitating my pitch. A few customers request my presence via other vendors. "Where's the hot, hot, hot guy?" they ask. In some instances, memorable pitches are treated like sacred family heirlooms, passed on from generation to generation of vendors. "Here it is!" one well-known beer vendor barks out inning after inning. According to him, a vendor started using that pitch in the 1970s when soda was going for sixty-five cents. The same vendor generates attention by basically telling people to move out of his way. "Excuse me! Pardon me!" he blares as he motors around the stadium. On the surface, he's being very polite, but he's really telling people to get the fuck out of his way.

As I evolve as a pretzel vendor, a friendly rivalry with my fellow pretzel vendor, the Hokie, takes shape. In the seventy-five minutes before the General's pre-game lecture, we sit together on Shea's concrete ramp and kill time. After that, though, it's a full-fledged pretzel war. During the day, the Hokie teaches elementary school. At the ballpark, he wants to capture pretzel supremacy. Once we hit the seats, we're in pitchers pitching a No No mode, not uttering a word, completely fixated on hawking. In *our* game, second is *last* place. By the eighth, a truce is called. We trade war stories as we head down to the Money Room to hand in our take. Hopefully, Heckle and Jeckle will be preoccupied when we get there. A few times, they have rudely interrupted my cash counting. "Are you short?" one of the brothers repeatedly asks, feigning concern as I count, breaking my concentration. By the time the Hokie and I are on the 7 train, we're back to not talking again. We're too beat. If I brought shorts along, I change quickly right there in the middle of the train. If there was a vendor locker room at Shea, I never found it.

When the the Hokie's parents visit the stadium, I make an addition to my pretzel call. "Smokin' not jokin'!" I pitch. When the Yankees come in for the annual Subway Series, when Shea is packed to the gills, I bring out the big guns—the Bazooka, an extra-large, rectangular metal canister that can hold three loads of pretzels (twenty pretzels per load). I just happened to notice the Bazooka on a shelf, looking as if it hadn't been used in years.

Two loads of pretzels are uncommon. Three loads are unheard of. After I inform Scorecard of my intention to utilize the previously retired Bazooka, he halts drawing his perfect Xs and looks up somewhat mystified. "He's going for the Bazooka!" Scorecard announces to no one in particular. "He's going for the Bazooka!" Everyone in the Pit appears to look up in awe—or perhaps they're just confused because they don't know what the Bazooka is, since that's the pet name that I've personally given it.

———

As the season wears on, the General continues to deliver impassioned pre-game State of the Unions, though they often don't pertain to me. Repeatedly, the General reminds beer vendors of these three rules:

1. You must ID every customer no matter how old they look.
2. Each customer is allowed two beers per transaction.
3. You can only sell to the bottom of the seventh or for two hours after the first pitch, whichever comes first.

Often, the General comes up with other rules for the beer vendors. For instance, one evening, the General forbids beer vendors from calling out "Last Call!" My take is that the General wants to make the stadium feel less like a saloon and more family friendly. Before another game, something else entirely weighs on the General's mind. Cryptically, he calls out vendor names and asks them to report to the front, where he stands atop a cafeteria table. Will these singled-out vendors be rewarded with $25 in cash for getting a perfect score on their secret shopper test? Or will they be demoted to the non-existent sunflower seeds? After a significant pause, once a sufficient amount of suspense has been created, the General explains that these vendors don't know how to wrap a dog properly. As punishment, these transgressors will be attending a mandatory dog-wrapping seminar.

—————

As early as August, the General reminds us that the playoffs are on the horizon, which means a full stadium packed with fair-weather fans who have money to blow. With that in mind, the General warns us not to do anything "stupid." In the next breath, he says that some vendors are getting "fat," which I interpret to mean that some vendors, probably beer vendors, are getting lazy. The General's word choice is reminiscent of Dean Wormer's famous quote from the movie *Animal House*: "Fat, drunk, and stupid is no way to go through life, son."

For me, the playoffs could pay huge dividends. After months of hawking pretzels and rappin' rhymes hard in the Cheap Seats, my hard work is being recognized. By invitation, I've taken and somehow passed the alcohol compliancy test. Now there's a chance that I could be doing the once unthinkable and rising to the pinnacle of the concessions chain. It all comes down to the last game of the regular season, all or nothing. If we win, the team gets playoffs—and I get the holy grail! If we lose, everyone gets nothing. The General treats this deciding game as a playoff game, ordering us to report three hours before first pitch. Inexplicably, I sell iced tea—not Long Island iced tea, unfortunately. I sell a lot of it, though ($5.50 per bottle). In the end, I lose because the Mets get blown out. By the eighth, with the stadium half empty, I cash out, and that's it for the season. No playoffs and no windfall.

On the cusp of the grail, I return to Shea the following year. In my sophomore season, the General regularly assigns me dogs, which are by no means a walk. Unfortunately, I'm no natural at dogs. Besides guiding the approximately forty-pound aluminum bin on my head as I negotiate thousands of stairs, I'm constantly maneuvering the bin from my head to the ground before proceeding with the assemblage of the dog. Often, I feel as if I'm in a Donkey Kong game. The worst part of dogs is a toss-up between dealing with the wrappers, which often slide out of the bin, and the sticky buns, which often seem as though they need to be opened with a wrench. I can't use my bare hands, so I have to open the bun with my fork. Needless to say, I've mangled my share of buns.

I mostly work the dogs on the Field, where Shea's aisles are extremely tight, making navigation tough, especially with the wide aluminum bin. In fact, one of the vendors, Double Play, a nervous, but likable, diminutive man, does not travel through the narrow aisles with his bin. Double Play keeps his bin at the top of the aisle and delivers the wrapped dogs to the customers. Double Play often says things twice. "Hot dog! Hot dog!" Double Play pitches. When Double Play isn't delivering, he seems to be monitoring his coworkers. A few times, Double Play attempts to adjust my name badge, to my annoyance. I hate my name badge. I feel no need to be on a first-name basis with my clientele. My credo is to sell the dog and run to the next sale.

While there are more tips on the Field, it does have a few strikes against it. For one, there's waiter service offered in the vast majority of seats that are directly behind home plate, an area that's off-limits to vendors. It's also ultra-competitive because the General usually packs this relatively small area with lots of dog vendors. There are only so many bucks, and only so much beef can be stomached. If you don't work fast, you'll get eaten alive. At the top of the sixth, dog sales practically come to a halt. Around the seventh or eighth, if it's remotely warm, fans want the cool stuff: ice cream or ices. For one game and one game only, the General puts me on double duty: dogs until the fifth before switching me over to ices. Immediately, I come up with a new, extremely popular pitch: "Ice! Ice! Baby!" You can't put a price tag on a kid's smile.

———

In all likelihood, it was Heckle and Jeckle who informed me that Scorecard was a goner. (Who else?) Allegedly, he had been stashing dogs on the sly, distributing them to a dog vendor, with whom he'd split the subsequent score. Scorecard wasn't the only goner. Pretzel Preparer hadn't run afoul of the law; he just wanted to keep a foul ball. Unfortunately for him, that's against stadium policy, and security demanded that Pretzel Preparer relinquish his souvenir immediately. At first, Pretzel Preparer refused. After a brief standoff, Pretzel Preparer reluctantly handed over the ball and was escorted out of the stadium.

———

As the season spirals toward its conclusion, the General once again mentions the playoffs and the inevitable but thus far elusive windfall that comes along with it. Once again, I brace myself for the holy grail, and once again, the season comes down to the final game. But it isn't any normal season finale. After this game, Shea will be demolished and replaced. For this final, pivotal game, I report three hours before first pitch. Just as I settle into my reading zone on the ramp, the General summons me, ordering me to hawk pretzels outside the stadium, where fans are already lining up to take a final walk on Shea's grass. While I appreciate the General's enthusiasm, I believe that his efforts are somewhat futile because it's before eleven in the morning and drizzling. I manage to sell a half-dozen or so before the General allows me in for his pre-game symposium. I expect a Grand Slam speech with loads of stadium nostalgia. I get anything but. Instead, the General announces that everyone won't be making the trip to the new stadium. He makes this pronouncement with such seriousness. It's as if he's denying admission to Noah's Ark. In his signature dramatic fashion, the General says that there are vendors among us who have chosen Scorecard's illicit path. After pausing a moment, the General requests that the unnamed vendors come clean immediately, so perhaps a negotiation and some sort of rehabilitation can begin. When the General finishes, the room falls silent.

No one steps forward.

The Mets blow the last game.

No holy grail!

9

World Cup for Roller Suckers

Perhaps I should have quit roller basketball while I was ahead, immediately after my full-body hug with TK. The following year, the Peace Frogs went up against Puerto Rico in the playoffs once again. We were down one Frog, our head Frog, TK, who had a conflict.

The game didn't own TK. TK owned the game.

Puerto Rico was out for blood and they were simply better. During the rematch, right from the jump, Superman made sure that he was in attendance.

After that game, an era ended. The next season, the Peace Frogs disbanded and not long after, Tom disbanded NIBBL. However, thanks to the unifying powers of the Internet, roller basketball played on, in such far-flung places as the Iberian Peninsula, Scandinavia, and the Middle East.

During the course of NIBBL's five-year or so life span, other roller hybrid sports emerged. While roller tennis and roller lacrosse never got off the ground, roller soccer progressed thanks to the fanatical efforts of its San Francisco–based creator Zack Phillips, who got the roller soccer brainstorm after kicking a pinecone in San Francisco's Golden Gate Park with his in-line skates. Phillips—whose hair is styled like a soccer ball with pentagonal lines and dyed red, white, and blue—had made the "pilgrimage" to New York and scrimmaged with NIBBLers, whom he considered to be the forefathers of the in-line hybrid sports movement. Subsequently, Phillips traveled the globe, kicking a soccer ball with his skates at soccer events and garnering followers, as well as strange looks, everywhere. With his unorthodox appearance, Phillips was often filmed with Uncle Sam's Army, the U.S. soccer team's traveling fan club.

Years after NIBBL disbanded, Phillips continued to keep us abreast of roller soccer's progress. He had already staged a few roller soccer World

Cups, including one in Paris, with teams coming from all over Europe. His ultimate dream was to hold the Roller Soccer World Cup in San Francisco, roller soccer's birthplace, featuring teams from every continent—plus a roller basketball tournament. For the latter, a Dutch team had agreed to come across the pond, and they were begging for NIBBL to reunite for one last match. Frankly, I felt like an 1980s synth band being asked to do a comeback performance for an episode of VH1's *Bands Reunited*. Unfortunately, Phillips got no takers from the NIBBL crowd—except one.

I reached out to the half dozen NIBBLers for whom I had contact information. I figured if I got a few, they'd get a few others and we'd have enough people to field a few teams. Spinner, the industrial artist who kept the practices from hitting a lull by reminding everyone that we were "burning daylight," was *in*. Besides Spinner, I wasn't having much luck. TK had a wedding. Tom, who had moved down south, had a leg injury and was saddled with other responsibilities, not to mention interests. Others, well, they just wanted no part of it. To complicate matters, we didn't have lodging. Personally, the whole production seemed kind of pricey for a non-reunion, where they were playing roller soccer, a sport we'd never played. With things looking bleak, I wrote an e-mail to Spinner.

> Spinner,
>
> I am having trouble getting two beds in the hostel—maybe one but not two. This is the last straw.
>
> I am ready to throw in the towel—and not go. If you want to call off your trip, I will pick up the cost of your plane ticket or what it costs to reschedule for a different trip. I feel bad—but a lot of people let me down. Let me know what your plans are.
>
> > Jon

Spinner's reply:

> Subject: Re: Quit freakin' whining, or I will skip out!
>
> Come on, Jon! We'll figure something out! If we have to find an all-night diner or skate all night, we'll do it. I think once we get there, the doors of benevolent empower-

ment will open wide for us and service ALL of our needs. So hang in there, and if I don't talk to you tonight, send along your flight information. Are you flying into Oakland on Continental?

NIBBL ON!!!!
Spinner

It was clear: Spinner *needed* this trip, and he was going—with or without me.

I was burning daylight!

If it was just me and him, so be it. Perhaps it was meant to be this way. We were both the guys that made the pass *before* the pass. I figured that we'd spend a few days in San Francisco and play some roller soccer, which couldn't be too tough. I'm a good skater.

Actually, I *was* a good skater.

I hadn't really skated in a while. But I had already conquered one hybrid sport. How hard could another one be?

⸻

When we arrive in San Francisco, we learn that the World Cup is coming apart at the seams. Just off the runway, we're greeted with this frantic e-mail from Phillips:

Subject: Bad news from Brazil and England

Hello team captains/organizers,

I just received news from Brazil. They kept trying until the last minute, but even with the help of politicians they were unable to get a visa.

Regarding England: Alvin recently suffered a knee injury playing regular soccer. Jana and Steve arrived in the USA a few days ago, but had to fly back to London due to a family emergency. As a result, Netherlands, England, and Germany will be combined into one team.

Even without Brazil and some of the key European players, the Roller Soccer World Cup kicks off. It's too late to cancel. The first day of the tournament, Spinner and I set out to the tournament's site, Treasure Island, which used to house a military base. Besides roller soccer enthusiasts, no one is there.

Phillips has somehow attracted an array of international teams: two teams from France (Paris and Marseilles), a team from Belgium, and players from Scandinavian countries, England, and Germany. Then, of course, there is Phillips and his fellow Bay Area players and the roller basketball refugees, Spinner and I. Phillips assigns Spinner and me to separate U.S. squads, and we're ready to roll. I'm not overly concerned. A while back, I had kicked a soccer ball with skates on, when Phillips visited our roller basketball practice.

Immediately, I learn that roller soccer is much more difficult than roller basketball. In roller soccer, there's no stability. Trying to kick a ball on skates is the perfect formula to falling on your ass and looking like a complete idiot. You have to roll with care or it's likely that your feet will roll out from under you. I figure I'll adjust to the new sport and I do, as I concentrate on one goal: not falling. As the games progress on the first day, things roll along just fine. We're not winning any games, but much, much more important, I'm not falling on my ass. That's OK. I'm really a former roller basketball player, and I have already won my world championship. I have nothing to prove. I'm just playing for, well, not to fall.

At some point in one of the games, which are being played on a hardwood surface surrounded by hockey boards, I find myself at mid-rink in the vicinity of the ball and a much taller opponent, Cherry. After a tentative start, my competitive juices have kicked in. We're both going for the ball. I have the angle and am going hard—Cherry or no Cherry. Cherry is a tough roller soccer veteran. Unfortunately, that doesn't stop her from losing her balance. Right before Cherry goes down, in a desperate attempt to balance herself, she wildly flings out her arms. Before she falls, one of her wrists firmly connects with my face. The blow itself might not have been that bad, but Cherry was wearing a metal wrist guard.

In short, I get clocked with a metal pipe.

Immediately, I fall on my ass—hard. Play is stopped. There's no blood but my face, not to mention the rest of my body, is awfully sore. For the duration, I play with a sore *everything*. My team, now in the losers' bracket after losing its first game, can't win a game the entire day.

Bruised and beaten, Spinner and I return to our lodging: a two-star, modest hotel. I'm thrilled to be there. I'm more beaten up than Spinner. His team had somehow managed to win a game, and he had even scored a goal, a rocket from way out and off to the side. Now, though, we're thinking about two things: rest and recuperation. We hit the beds with a vengeance. (By the way, Spinner isn't complaining about the lodging that I had procured.) I take a few aspirin, ice my face, and fall asleep. Hours later, Spinner shows up with dinner for two.

"Thanks, Spin."

"You all right?"

"I think I broke it?"

"Your nose?"

"My ass."

"You're just getting older," he says with a laugh.

"I am not!" I reply back, annoyed. "A roller soccer Amazon hit me in the face with a steel bar!"

We don't say much after that. In the dark, we scarf down our food and drift off.

The next day, I'm still sore but ready to give roller soccer another go. Unfortunately, my winless team is deflated and continues to be outplayed. The European teams have more of a knack for roller soccer. There's one kid from Belgium who's particularly good. When I say kid, I do mean kid. At about 5 feet on wheels, he's approximately fourteen years old. His parents have chaperoned him across the world, so he can participate in the World Cup. He's quick to the ball and falling down doesn't bother him one iota. With ease, he skates around flailing bodies. When I realize I traveled across the country to get beaten by a fourteen-year-old, I'm no longer disappointed that the World Cup is so off the beaten path on a deserted island and not in a central location with heavy pedestrian traffic, like say Ghirardelli Square. Now, I'm grateful that the tournament is taking place in the boondocks. I don't need an audience for this.

There's one other thing that I mind more than the soreness. As our losses become increasingly lopsided, one malcontent on our team, Beckham, becomes increasingly agitated, and he attempts to coach us.

Beckham's style veers overwhelmingly toward critical as opposed to constructive.

Lighten up, Beckham. We're in the losers' bracket of the Roller Soccer World Cup. Deal with it and don't take it out on the rest of us. My ass is broken! Practice for next year and maybe you won't feel like a roller sucker!

Meanwhile, Spinner's squad is faring much, much better. His team has won a few games and is on the verge of winning another. If Spinner can convert a penalty kick, his team will advance to the next round. After traveling across the country to a roller basketball reunion that never happened, I feel that it's poetic justice to some degree. When the whistle blows, Spinner dribbles toward the net and boots the ball. I'm ready to yell GOAL! Sadly, Spinner's shot doesn't have a prayer, and the ball slowly rolls off to the side. It's over. Both our teams are out.

Before the day ends, Phillips places a few baskets on the rink for a roller basketball scrimmage. It's good to be back shooting on wheels (and not kicking things and falling down). Compared to roller soccer, roller basketball is a graceful ballet. Unfortunately, right after it starts, it ends. Phillips has a ton of roller soccer games to get in, so we're quickly rushed off the court.

Our last night, Spinner and I engage in our favorite vacation activity. As we rest and recuperate, we watch the romantic comedy *No Reservations*, which stars actors Catherine Zeta-Jones and Aaron Eckhart. It's about chefs who are so wrong for one another, they're . . . Well, I don't want to be a spoiler. It's the only thing on and turns out to be thoroughly enjoyable thanks to Spinner, who does some wonderful commentary, which carries us through to the closing credits.

———

I never play roller soccer again. However, whenever it's on, I do watch *No Reservations*.

Spinner and I will always have San Francisco.

10

Extra Innings

Sergeant Pepper vended year-round, but Pepper was no Heckle and
Teckle. He was just struggling to hold on. Like Theckle, who had
earned somewhat of a cult following by pitching the name of a certain
item *backwards*, Pepper was one of the ballpark's eternal eccentrics. Pepper was prone to standing still in the stands, staring off into the abyss.
Late one winter evening, Pepper was coming home from an event, and
he was in distress, at least in part because of his precarious job status.

In this respect, Pepper was not alone. A fair number of vendors had
experience with limited job prospects. Before they worked the stands,
some vendors had been in the corporate sector. When they were down-
sized and unable to return to the corporate life, they became reliant on
hawking. In his quiet way, the General, who from what I understand, has
a successful career in addition to vending, was aware of this situation,
and he seemed to get a certain level of satisfaction in providing positions
for displaced individuals (though I'd never heard him actually articulate
this). During moments of crisis, such as the time when one of the senior
vendors got seriously injured in a car accident, the General delivered this
simple message to us in his own unique way: you're not alone.

It's a part-time gig, but the General was a full-time protector.

Unfortunately, there were things that were beyond the General's control. In vending, things are drastically changing. New, more compact stadiums with fewer seats are becoming the norm. Increasingly, stadiums
are using waiter service. Among hawkers, it's an open secret: vending is
slowly but surely being phased out. This must have been devastating for
Pepper. In the past few decades, there had been one constant in Pepper's
life: no matter what, there'd be 162 baseball games a year (Yankees and

Mets), plus all the other miscellaneous events. Pepper was worried that it all might be ending. Also, I heard that he was depressed over the loss of a family member. That late winter evening, Pepper stepped in front of a moving train. A night or two later, a moment of silence was held in Madison Square Garden's vending room.

———

A few months later, a sparkling new Citi Field opens with lots of fanfare. At orientation, the vending force is informed that it's responsible for "making memories."

On Opening Day, I am hustling dogs hard on the Field, and the place is packed with lots of fair-weather fans. I'm working extra-hard because dogs take special care, and I'm no natural. Around the seventh or eighth, which is when dog sales are on life support, I hit an aisle and an older woman, probably not a regular fan, turns to me. "And now you come," she tells me dismissively in a heavy Long Island accent, implying that I've been on a personal mission to avoid serving her.

As far as vendors are concerned, Citi's no field of dreams, at least compared to Shea, which might've been a sprawling dump, but was good for vendors. First, the new building is more compact, making it easier for customers to access concession stands, where there are large monitors so that fans won't miss a single out. As far as the actual concessions, Citi offers a plethora of options, including more upscale fare (sushi and entrées from such well-regarded restaurants such as Shake Shack and Blue Smoke) as well as several lounge-type areas that are strictly off-limits to vendors. In general, Citi encourages fans to walk around and serve themselves rather than stay planted in their seats. At Citi, baseball feels like it's being played in a mall. (At Shea, there was nowhere to roam, and to some degree it felt like baseball in an incinerator. Some fans claim to prefer Shea, and they wear T-shirts that say "I'm calling it Shea.") To exacerbate the situation, the waiter service area has been extended. The Bernie Madoff Section, my name for the area behind home plate, features oversized cushioned seats. Behind this ridiculously expensive area, there are even more ridiculously expensive private suites. A few times, I spot Jerry Seinfeld standing on the deck of his suite. At Citi, where they need *half* the number of vendors than they used at Shea, the Cheap Seats are *not* so cheap.

At Citi, some of the Pit preparers can't count. I have to be extra-careful that the correct number of items are inserted into my pouch. (If I go out short, I'm picking up the tab.) We can't complain about the incorrect counting. When someone does, the General reminds us that there are several vendors who are also counting challenged. Often, the perpetually nervous Double Play turns counting into an extra-tense affair. "Count it! Count it!" Double Play repeats as he intently watches the pretzels being inserted into the pouches. Except for being so damn nervous, Double Play is a sweet man. In stark contrast, Dykstra, a longtime Pit veteran, is dangerous. Former Met Lenny Dykstra used to crash into walls. In the small, congested Pit, Dykstra pushes and bumps into vendors as he mumbles to himself, never offering an apology.

By August, the Mets are out of playoff contention. If nothing else, people turn out to see Citi and chow on California rolls.

While the Mets slide, I'm winning my bout against the blank page. Slowly but surely, I start to piece together my manuscript.

———

By the following March, I'm ready to step up to the plate and approach publishers. I'm not quitting vending, though. The physical labor is an adrenaline rush and during the three hours in the stands, I have plenty of time to meditate over my thoughts. And, of course, I enjoy listening to the General. It never gets old.

During our pre-season meeting, the General doesn't have good news: pre-season ticket sales aren't strong and some of the vending force might not be needed. Opening Day, a virtual holiday when hope springs eternal, is far from a sellout, and some fans are angry, in no mood to purchase overpriced concessions.

Early in the season, the General turns his attention to an entirely different matter: an alarming number of dogs are unaccounted for, and the General says that he strongly suspects that there's a dog thief in our midst. I don't pay much mind because I'm selling pretzels, which are now holeless, bulky sticks that cost $6.25. When I inform customers of this price, most accept it. Others, however, seem visibly shaken.

"It's cheaper than Vegas," I say in a consolatory tone to many a customer, which often placates them. But not always.

"We're *not* in Vegas," one lady tells me. Good point.

Worse, the pretzel's calorie count is now printed on my badge. In one horizontal pretzel, there are exactly 497 calories, which draws endless, annoying commentary from *non-buyers*. Calorie talk in the stands is nothing new. Often, I overhear fans discussing how many calories I'm burning working the stands. I'm privy to as much calorie talk during a game as I would during an exercise infomercial.

———

A few months later, the Yankees travel cross-town for the annual Subway Series. For this sold-out series, the General has asked for vendor referrals. Some vendors discourage this because more vendors equals more competition, which leads to less pay. Despite the efforts of a few, the General does get a few neophytes. The Rookie, a masculine girl, draws pretzels in the the Not So Cheap Seats. It's a decent assignment because pretzels are now transported in a light foam bag (without a Sterno) and the steps are gentler at Citi. Also, of course, the Rookie has a full house at her disposal. Despite all this, the Rookie looks uncomfortable and clueless, so I try to give her the primer that no one gave me.

Walk up every step!

Be loud!

Show your item!

Hold on to your cash!

I never said vending was physics. Of course, that's a large part of its beauty.

Unfortunately, for the first game of the Subway Series, the regular pretzel preparer is absent and that leads to long, frustrating delays. (The ancient furnace had been retired with Shea's demise, replaced with a microwave.) After I finally sell my first load, the Rookie is back in the Pit, but she's out of her bumblebee uniform. She's done. This gig could be for anyone, but it's not for everyone.

The General saves some of his most impassioned pre-game State of the Unions for the Yankees. As usual, he enters and stands on a ramp, so that he can view his people, many of whom are related to one another. (There are several sets of brothers and a few father and son duos.) Immediately after the General appears, the vendors swarm toward him, a flock of yellow jackets hovering toward their king bee. He always starts the same. "Ladies and gentlemen, welcome to another game at Citi Field . . ." Then, for special games such as this, in his understated but utterly compelling way, the General tells us that we're being given an *opportunity*, a very rare opportunity, and we should take advantage of it. The subtext of his speech: *It doesn't matter who you are, where you have been, or where you will be, tonight you have the opportunity to have a lucrative evening GO FOR IT!*

For the second game with the Yankees, I request pretzels again. It's routine, drama free. But to my surprise, I get the holy grail! I'm not getting the nod because of my hawking acumen. The General needs bodies. I wear two special buttons that say this:

- "We I.D."
- "WE CARD EVERYONE REGARDLESS OF AGE. . . .
  SERVICE LIMIT: TWO ALCOHOLIC BEVERAGES PER
  CUSTOMER PER TRANSACTION."

In the Not So Cheap Seats, I'm in demand, but getting fans to show me their IDs is a real pain. People, men in particular, just don't want to readily hand it over to me. (Women are often flattered.) I can't really blame the guys. Basically, I'm a cop with no power in a bumblebee getup. Consequently, each sale is somewhat of a brief standoff.

Besides this obstacle, sales are solid. In fact, I can't pour fast enough. That's the key with beer: the pour. Get the beer out of the can as fast as possible. In most cases, I pour, then squeeze the can, forcing whatever remaining liquid out as fast as possible. Many beer vendors use can openers to punch a hole in the can to expedite the pour. A few pour two at a time. Some beer vendors have been known to do the quick pour, not squeezing out every last drop. And a beer vendor or two have been known to gain an advantage in moving product by engaging in a practice called "barring," which is camping out in the corridor, not working the seats, encouraging customers to form a line. Barring is against the rules, but it happens.

Immediately, I learn that beer customers are different from other customers. They're aggressive and often boisterous. As I'm pouring, squeezing, and pondering, my world gets turned upside down. As I'm leaning over to serve a customer, my beer box, which is sitting on one of the stairs, unexpectedly tips over and full cans scatter under seats. During previous games when I witnessed a customer drop their beer, it was always a sad moment, even wake worthy. Perhaps I'd stop and offer my condolences. Now, however, I'm experiencing a completely different emotion: horror. Frantically searching for cans, I do a 180, and I see an unforgettable sight: one lone can bouncing—yes, actually bouncing—down the stairs. As I helplessly watch it, I feel as though the entire stadium has ceased paying attention to the game and is focused on this lone can's descent. Finally, they're watching *my* game—but at the worst possible moment. If I could dive after the bouncing can, I would, but it's too late. When the can finally hits the bottom of the aisle, it erupts, shooting a stream of suds about six feet into the air. I hear a dull roar from behind me. I continue my mad scramble to retrieve the cans under the seats. Thankfully, one or two kindhearted fans point me toward them. After picking up the damaged can at the bottom of the stairs, I disappear into the corridor.

I need a fresh start.

Fortunately, there are plenty of aisles that didn't witness the episode, and I'm back in business immediately. It's hard not to succeed with this pumped, full house. Just as I'm making headway, my two-hour beer selling window is closing. In a desperate attempt to unload my remaining beers, I play the corners, hitting one of the far ends of the stadium, hoping that it has been neglected. Fortunately, my hunch is correct and a flurry of hands holding passports go up. They're Austrian tourists, and they desperately want beer! Baseball is a big tourist attraction. But before I can get to them, a couple, both wearing Yankee shirts, wave me down. However, Mr. and Mrs. Yankee are having trouble locating their IDs. So with my time window close to expiration, I service a few other customers who are a few stairs up. After I pour and squeeze about a half-dozen, I observe that the clock has struck twelve, so to speak, and that I'm over the two-hour limit. It's over. I desperately want to service the healthy

Austrian contingent, not to mention Mr. and Mrs. Yankee—but can't. If I'm caught by the alcohol compliance officers or one of the video monitors that I'm not sure actually exists, I'll face the General's wrath. No doubt, he'll banish me from beer and probably sentence me to sunflower seeds for, well, eternity. With no other option, I walk away from the Austrians, who are incredulous. Situated high up and in the middle of the aisle, they can't show me their inner-hooligan tendencies. However, Mr. and Mrs. Yankee, who are right on the aisle, have a clear shot at me. I attempt to explain: *I cannot under any circumstances whatsoever . . . I'm just a lowly concessions hawker . . . I was supposed to be selling pretzels!*

"Scumbag!" Mr. Yankee yells at me before I can finish. As I descend down the stairs, I steal a glance at Mr. and Mrs. Yankee, who have venom in their eyes. Prior to the series, in his pre-game State of the Union, the General had prepared us for such scenarios, imparting us with this simple message: *Do not under any circumstances engage.* Just as the General instructed, I continue my descent down the stairs, staring straight ahead, my back to Mr. and Mrs. Yankee, who continue their diatribe.

As I walk back to the Pit, I learn that a reprieve has been granted. The beer-selling deadline has been extended by thirty minutes. There's one catch: we can't sell in the seats, only in the corridor. I'm not sure what the rationale for this condition is. Perhaps it's a sobriety test: fans must be able to walk down the steps before they can purchase a beer. With the extension granted, I head back to where I was just verbally accosted and beg a security guy to get the customers to come down to me. One of the rowdy Austrians is the first to reach me, and he promptly shoves his passport at me, ordering sixteen beers. Yes, sixteen. I politely explain that it's two per customer and that his fellow countrymen have to personally show me their IDs. "I've been drinking since I was fourteen!" the Austrian bellows in his heavy accent. Meanwhile, I'm surrounded by customers, and I start pouring and squeezing as fast as I possibly can. I need to concentrate, but a Yankees fan wants to discuss the vendor hierarchy and the long odyssey I've taken to get to the Everest of the concessions ladder. "You've worked hard to get to this level," he tells me as I squeeze. Unlike many Yankee fans, who are arrogant and have an overdeveloped sense of entitlement, he's polite and patient. For some reason, I feel obligated to come clean on my true ranking in the hawking hierarchy.

Eventually, in so many words, I come clean: *I'm not really a beer man! I'm a pretzel guy! I'm an imposter!*

And the very next night, I'm back to selling pretzels on the Field, where I'm alarmed to find *intruders*. Unfortunately, the waiter service area has been extended beyond the Bernie Madoff Section, and it now includes much of the Field. As I hawk, I watch the waiters, who wear conspicuous blue shirts, take orders with their handheld mechanical devices and sit in the aisles as they wait to be beckoned by fans. During this game, I have a memorable back-and-forth with an immaculately dressed fan. Actually, I don't know if he's a fan. He probably doesn't go to many games at all, just special events like the Subway Series. He's not a fan. He's a customer. There's a difference.

"How you doing?" the customer asks.

"Good."

"Really?"

"Yeah, *really*." I'm doing all right. It's a Subway Series game, and sales are robust, which makes the night relatively painless and somewhat lucrative. "Why?"

"Well, it's a Sunday night and you're selling pretzels."

Thanks for your input, *guy*.

With the Blue Shirts taking away our customers, some vendors actually request to work in the Not So Cheap Seats, where there are no Blue Shirts and thus less competition. Not yet, anyway.

———

At some point during my tenure, there's a high-profile exposé on stadium food. I didn't see the report. As I understand it, the Health Department doesn't seem to have the highest regard for stadium cuisine. None of my customers seem to care about the report, though. Over the course of the season, only one customer actually mentions it. Ironically, every game, several bring up the exorbitant price of the pretzels (now up to $6.50), which actually cost more than a Bud.

Around this same time, in a highly publicized incident, a disgruntled flight attendant quits his job by cracking open a beer before sliding down the emergency ramp of his just-landed plane. While the General doesn't specifically mention the incident, it becomes clear that he wants to discourage any similar rebellious acts from his staff. The General tells us to utilize extreme caution, and warns that our actions are being scrutinized more than ever. (Indeed, with the newly installed computer system, the General is able to tell when we go out with each load.) My interpretation of these statements: the General appears to be aware that every vendor has their breaking point.

A few times, I've been close to the breaking point myself. After one Sunday scorcher, I am faint from heat and exhaustion, and I practically go over the edge. In fact, I experience a carbohydrate massacre—a carbassacre. I devour not one but two 497-calorie pretzels and one piece of fried dough topped with sugar (500 calories). When it comes to acts of vendor gluttony, I'm not alone. During a concert when sales are slow, the Hokie eats something like seventeen leftover dogs—and lives to tell about it.

———

One day, the General finally bags his dog thief. During a day game, he goes into action. Accompanied by a police officer, the General approaches Zeus, the legendary dog vendor. Promptly, Zeus drops his bin and makes a run for it. *Say it ain't so, Zeus. Say it ain't so.*

Zeus isn't the only one to depart the circus. Late in the season, I'm in mid-game form. "Hot! Hot! Hot! I blare as I always do. I scan the seats, up and down, back and forth, and there he is: Lifer, sitting in the seats, out of uniform, conspicuously silent. We lock eyes, and he gives me a melancholy smile. I do something that I rarely do during a game: I stop. Vending is a solo affair, but Lifer had gone out of his way to give me a few vending pointers.

"Where you been?"

"I was fired."

"What!?" I yell. Unintentionally, I'm conversing in my vendor voice.

"They told me that I can come back next year if I sober up."

"So come back next year."

"I've lost my seniority."

If Lifer returned, he'd be selling the worst items in the worst places, at least technically.

"So you'll get it back, eventually."

Lifer just shakes his head.

There are other casualties.

Dykstra pushed the wrong vendor in the Pit and was finally pushed into retirement. Hackett just couldn't get to the stadium on time and was dismissed. The Genius, the Oliver Stone of cotton candy, was let go for making inappropriate remarks while pitching his item.

Heckle and Jeckle's reign finally ended. One of them had mocked a fellow vendor's arrest to a senior-level vendor. Immediately, the guilty brother was suspended. Instead of serving the suspension, Heckle and Jeckle both quit and left town. If they weren't going to vend, there was nothing left for them.

Eventually, the Hokie stopped showing up. Graduate school and a fiancée were on his agenda.

While I don't miss Heckle and Jeckle, I miss Zeus. Zeus had charisma and even some class. When Derek Jeter walked past us before a Subway Series game, a vendor heckled him, and Zeus promptly ordered the vendor to can it. When I was assigned beer, Zeus informed me that it was vendor etiquette to allow the Professor, the senior emeritus vendor, to load up first. Sometimes as I climb the steps, I imagine Zeus having his post-game beer in the Pit, on the house, of course. When you're walking stairs for three hours, your mind wanders. It's one of the perks of the job.

Why do baseball managers wear uniforms?

The First Pitch: It has been cheapened. Most can't even make it . . .

What exactly is a Hokie?

What kind of man wears skinny jeans?

I prefer a good rain delay over forced elevator chatter any day . . .

Eddie Money is underappreciated . . .

And sometimes I imagine that I'm someone else, somewhere else, during some other time. I'm a soldier in Vietnam, walking through a swamp in the jungle. My bin, which I'm holding over my head, is a rifle . . . I'm a gondolier in Venice . . . And sometimes, perhaps similar to Pepper, I'm walking around wondering what it all means . . .

Inevitably, though, something jars me back to reality. It could be a close call with a foul ball, or it could be something else entirely. During a night game, I'm going through yet another sale. I'm frustrated, and it has nothing to do with how much I'm selling. I've begun to take my proposal to publishing types. While I'm getting some positive comments, I'm not getting any bites. They're nice, but they're still rejections. You can hit a perfect line drive, but if it's caught, it's still an out. Suddenly, the customer's friend turns around, and I'm face-to-face with someone who I *don't* want to serve. I had the misfortune of playing in a few basketball (conventional, not roller) games with the Baller, a nasty, entitled, trash-talking player. He would make a great Yankee fan! In general, I don't enjoy serving acquaintances. Often, they spot me in my bumblebee attire, conclude that I've fallen on tough times, and act awkward. As far as the beauty of vending, they are clueless. During previous games, I had spotted the Baller and went out of my way to stay clear. Now, I'm stuck serving his friend, and the Baller is talking to me as if we're cool. But the conversation is one-sided because I don't utter a word and keep my face down, feigning concentration.

> A legendary vendor signs off to less-than-affable customers with this closing, curt comment: "Have a nice day!" he says defiantly. On the surface, he's being polite. In reality, he's saying, "Go fuck yourself!"

Finally, I turn to the Baller, our faces just inches apart, and I rudely interrupt him. "Do you want a pretzel?" I ask pointedly. According to the General's unwritten handbook, it's the only reply I have in my arsenal.

As another season winds down, I think of a memorable encounter with the General. We had worked a double header the previous day, and everyone's feeling it. Many had opted to just stay away from Shea. When I get my assignment card, I see that the General had written a special note on it: "See me." This can't be good. Thus far into my tenure, I had limited one-on-one contact with the General. Once he took fault with the penmanship on my vendor card. Another time, when I was stuck with cotton candy in the Cheap Seats, he examined one of my bushels and found it to be imperfect, through no fault of my own, and promptly ordered me to replace it.

I approach the General cautiously and show him my card. He takes it and looks down. Nervously, I wait as I ponder whether sunflower seeds are in my immediate future. Finally, the General turns to me. "Well, I kind of gave you what you wanted," he says finally, before breaking into a broad smile. The General doesn't smile often. Even when we sing him happy birthday or give him a standing ovation at orientation, he doesn't really smile that much. Now, however, he is definitely smiling. It's a smile that he reserves for very special occasions, like when he's reunited with a former vendor.

I had requested pretzels in the lower mezzanine, which I'd dubbed the Pasture because its steps are shaded and easy. It's where older vendors are put out to pasture. After the double header, that's exactly how I feel. Instead, the General has given me the Pasture *and* the Field—all to myself. I am basically being given the key to Willy Wonka's Chocolate Factory, and the General knows it. He has given me a "monopoly," a term he uses. Ordinarily, about four pretzel vendors would cover these two areas. Yes, the General is short on vendors, but this is his way of acknowledging my efforts, and he wants to deliver the good news to me personally. "I know you can do it," he tells me.

During the game, my legs were dead, but I persevered. Earning the General's approval was a big W.

11
Racing up the Empire State Building

After the season, I set my sights on the Empire State Building Run-Up, a race up the skyscraper. Unfortunately, the number of participants in this race is limited and admission is no guarantee. When I apply, I state my credentials. Besides my one unremarkable New York City marathon finish, I inform the Empire State race entry committee about hustling up and down thousands of steps at the ballpark and nabbing the record for selling the most pretzels in a single game at Citi Field. On a Mother's Day Sunday, I sold 180 pretzels at $6.50 a pop. It was cloudy and cool, ideal pretzel-hawking weather. Unfortunately, there's no plaque for this record, and it's not listed *anywhere*. No one knows about it—except me and the Empire State Building race entry committee. Also unfortunately, they don't seem to really care, because they don't get back to me, at least not immediately. I start training anyway, attempting to simulate the Empire run. Since I don't have access to a skyscraper, I run up and down my eleven-story building eight times, two or three times a week. (It takes about twenty minutes.) After weeks of running (and walking) up and down stairs, I feel prepared, kind of. I just need a race number.

Mere weeks before the race, surprisingly, I get the thumbs-up e-mail. I'm in the race—well, kind of. It's actually the preliminary race for non-professional stair runners. Because, apparently, there are *professional* stair runners out there.

Just before nine in the morning on the first Tuesday in February, I'm in the lobby of the Empire State Building. As workers rush to elevators to get to their cubicles, I step up to the starting line. With about a hundred competitors, I'm about to run up the 1,576 stairs to the eighty-sixth floor. I'm somewhat prepared but anxious about the claustrophobic stairwell, which I've never seen. Attempting to avoid unsettling thoughts, I strike up a conversation with one of the racers, a guy wearing black biker shorts.

"Take it easy until the twentieth floor," Lance Armstrong says. "You don't want to crash early."

"Have you ever done this before?" another male racer interjects.

"No," says Lance.

Indeed, most of us have never done this before—and that's exactly why we're doing it.

Finally, it's starting time, 9 a.m. "Ready," the starter announces. HONK! A loud horn sounds—and we're off.

———

Running up buildings is nothing new. Since the turn of the twentieth century, building or tower running has been around, according to Michael Reichetzeder, a veteran tower runner, who runs Towerrunning, the sport's unofficial organizing body. When it comes to running up buildings, Reichetzeder, who resides in Vienna, *is* the man. According to Reichetzeder, it's rumored that runners raced up the Eiffel Tower as early as 1905.

The Empire State Building started its race in 1978. That same year, Toronto's CN Tower began its annual race as well. Now, Reichetzeder estimates that there are about two hundred tower races a year, and he says that the sport is gradually gaining acceptance in the traditional sports world. For instance, in 2010, tower running's unofficial World Cup held in Torre Colpatria (Bogotá) was recognized by the Colombian national athletic federation.

———

After the horn, we run underneath the starting line banner and make a sharp turn toward the building's stairwell. Everything's civilized. I'm in the preliminary or the warm-up race for amateurs. In the later heat, when the professionals enter the Empire's tight stairwell, it's ultra-competitive, somewhat akin to running with the bulls. As the pros jockey for position, it's not uncommon for runners to hit the ground and be trampled on, at least partially.

After fifteen or so strides, I get to the narrow stairwell's door, where runners are anxiously shuttling in, one at a time. In the dusty, tight stairwell, I'm surrounded by limbs. I maintain a steady pace on the inside lane, hitting every stair (because it's lower impact). I'm behind a female racer, who's alternating between nailing every stair and every other. Meanwhile, a few people pass me on my right. I probably could've passed a few people myself, but it's just the beginning, and I'm conserving energy. I want to do well. Even more than that, I want to avoid hyperventilating and stopping.

About the fourteenth floor, still behind the alternating stepper, I'm alarmed by a strange noise from my stomach. The toast I had eaten a few hours earlier is talking. Puking in itself wouldn't be so bad. However, puking in a narrow stairwell possibly on a fellow competitor certainly would be. Fortunately, my stomach shuts up and I get to the twentieth floor, where a race worker directs me to exit and switch stairwells. While I'm prepared for this course change, the male competitor in front of me, who's hooked into his earphones, is not, and he continues to run up the *wrong* stairwell. After I yell at him, he finally stops. On the twentieth floor, there are tables with pyramids of cups of water, which I run right past. Of course, I want water, but I know better than to indulge thanks to the advice of a race veteran, who had warned me beforehand, "You can't drink and breathe at the same time!"

After the twentieth floor, the pack spreads out, and I acclimate myself to the design of the new stairwell: each flight is one long continuous stretch of stairs. (On the previous stairwell, each flight was made up of two relatively short stretches separated by a small landing.) I prefer the new design, which allows me to find a steadier rhythm. Somewhat similar to a rower, I use both railings to pull myself up. Reichetzeder had told me that professional building runners often practice different rail techniques. During my training, I had resisted using the railings because I wanted to build stamina. As I row up the stairs, a female racer, who's pulling on just one of the railings quite effectively, passes me. Immediately, I switch to her method. Staying tight on the inside lane, I pull on the rail as if I'm a mountain climber pulling a rope, one hand in front of the other. As my arms go forward, my legs follow. With this seemingly more effective method, I pass a few people, including someone who had previously passed me, and reach the sixty-fifth floor, the site of the second checkpoint. As expected, my legs are heavy and I'm short of breath. I'm not wearing a watch and they're not calling out times, so I have no idea how fast I'm going. When I get to the top, I'll get to the top.

In the homestretch, I feel like I have some gas left. I contemplate breaking off from my rope tow method that's served me so well and gunning it. Right before I do just this, I pass one of my fellow male runners on one of the landings. He's a cautionary tale. Slumped over with his hands on his knees, he's desperately gasping. With that sight, I stay with what had gotten me this far. As I work my way up the final flights, the air becomes considerably cooler. The Empire State's security people offer encouragement, and one even notifies me of the time after I request it. "It's nine twenty," he says. If his watch is correct, I'm way behind schedule. I had been hoping to finish the race in fifteen minutes or so. I immediately regret not training harder. Then I remember that I *hate* training. With the fifteen-minute pipe dream dashed, I settle for not puking, not fainting, and just finishing with an average time—certainly not first but certainly not last.

Finally, I reach the eighty-sixth floor, exit the stairwell, and run down a carpet toward the Empire State's observation deck. On the flat surface, my legs are like Jell-O. "Be careful, it's slippery outside," one of the race volunteers warns me. "It's sleeting." On the observation deck, I'd hoped to be rewarded with a glorious view of the city skyline. Instead, I observe absolutely nothing. A heavy fog has blanketed the city. As I run the final yards to the finish, I embrace the cold sleet. My finishing time is 20:51. For comparison's sake, Paul Crake, an Australian cyclist who holds the record, ran up the Empire State in 9:33. Sadly, a few years ago, Crake was paralyzed in a cycling accident. Now, Thomas Dold is the reigning Empire State champion, having won the competition six times in a row.

Immediately after crossing the finish, I'm awarded a medal. At the finish, I stick around, congratulating fellow competitors as they come in. Due to lack of space at the summit, race volunteers order us to immediately go downstairs.

Fortunately, they demand that we take the elevator.

12

Spring Training

As far as vending, I had pulled a Brett Favre too many times.

In this respect, I'm not alone. Vendors always talk about quitting. Before I hung up my tray, there was one thing that I had vowed to work: spring training. I'd heard that it was a must. If you're a college basketball player, you want to play in Pauley Pavilion or Allen Fieldhouse. If you're a vendor, you want to work spring training.

After seasons of procrastination, I finally report to City of Palms Park in Fort Myers, Florida, the Boston Red Sox spring training complex, for a matinee. In the venue's sole vending pit, an elderly expeditor seems skeptical of my abilities. "Have you ever done it before?" asks Iron Man, whose job is to hand the vendors heavy trays of water and soda. "Yeah," I respond, keeping it simple. I'm not sure that Iron Man actually heard my reply. As I later confirmed, you have to speak directly into Iron Man's ear for him to hear you. "What do you want, peanuts or water?" another worker asks me. I had already spotted another elderly gentleman selling nuts in the corridor. In the warm climate, where the vendors are allowed to wear shorts (something the General absolutely forbids), I figure that everyone must need water, even at $4.75 a pop. City of Palms only uses ten or so vendors. Perhaps six of those hawk the holy grail, which I have no chance at nabbing because I'm the tourist vendor. Gladly, I accept water. Promptly, Iron Man removes a tray of twenty-four 30-ounce waters from the fridge and pours ice cubes on top of the tray. My tray comes with a cushioned strap to place around my back. However, I always go strapless because I find straps to be awkward. With the tray on my head, I head out, and a few moments later, I shoot out of the tunnel and into the stands, back to playing *my* game. Since it's somewhat warm, I'm prepared to be busy. I'm pumped. I'm at spring training!

As excited as I am, I do have some reservations. I'm all too familiar with the dark side of water. It can be a bitch because it's heavy and people aren't particularly thrilled with being overcharged for what's essentially tap water. In mid-season form, I can really belt it out. "WAAATER! Waater! Waater!" I transform myself into a one-man opera, often able to garner the attention of players on the field. Now, inexplicably, when I open my trap, almost nothing comes out to my absolute horror. I can barely manage a croak. I haven't a clue what's wrong. Perhaps it was the early morning flight. Is it a case of early season jitters? The drastic change in the weather? I don't know. I guess it's fitting. I'm at Spring Training, working the kinks out along with the players.

The stairs at City of Palms, an intimate, single-level ballpark surrounded by Palm trees, are gentle and don't venture high. There's one main, wide aisle that encircles the park, which can be difficult to navigate because it's often congested with standing-room-only spectators. "Excuse me, pardon me!" I bark repeatedly as I weave through the fans. On the surface, I'm being very polite. But I'm really telling people this: Get the fuck out of my way! Every game at City of Palms sells out. A fellow vendor tells me that the Sox can squeeze as many as nine thousand fans into the place.

For my spring training debut, I hit the stands early, too early, an hour before the game, when the place is relatively empty. It's a rookie move. Experienced vendors want to wait until the place fills up, so they don't waste energy on empty seats. However, it's a calculated move on my part. I want to soak up every second of spring training. After an hour of wandering around without much action, things pick up. Every time I'm waved down, I lift the tray off my head, bring it down to the ground, remove and serve water, and collect cash. More often than not, fans tip me the quarter. After the transaction, I raise the tray back up atop my head.

No off-season training program can replicate vending. Besides the physical adjustment and my inability to yell, I'm experiencing equipment malfunction. I'm selling water out of a beer tray, which has a firm Styrofoam holder for *beer* bottles. Unfortunately, the holes are not quite large enough for my water bottles. Somehow, Iron Man has squeezed water bottles into the tight holes. Each time I remove a water bottle, it's somewhat of a struggle. When the bottle finally comes free, a loud suction noise follows, similar to a cork being unplugged from a wine bottle. After finally selling a tray, I return to the Pit and wait, where Iron Man is holding court.

"How old are you, Iron Man? Eighty?" one of the vendors asks him.

"I'm eighty-three!" Iron Man says proudly. Iron Man is a young eighty-three. Here, at City of Palms, we're all young. In part, that's why we're all here.

I pay for my load and reload. As I head out the door with the tray of water bottles atop my head, I hear Iron Man boasting about his alcohol consumption. "I drink three glasses of wine every night, and I'm *not* talking cups. I'm talking *glasses!*" he boasts. Eleven months out of the year, Iron Man is retired. In March, City of Palms is *his* house!

At City of Palms, the vast majority of the fans are around Iron Man's age. In regard to sales, this turns out to be a good thing. Rather than make the walk to one of the concession stands in the corridor, many of the customers prefer to stay put in their seats. Surprisingly, very few complain about the exorbitant price of the water. However, there are a few exceptions. Most notably, I get a complaint or two from *non-buyers*, fans who are passing down a water to a fellow customer.

"How much is that?" they ask rhetorically, acting as though they didn't actually see my conspicuous price badge. They want to hear themselves and hear me actually say the price. By having me say it, they're doing what they intended: making me pay! They want me to be ashamed. Frankly, I'm too frustrated from having no voice and removing the waters to be ashamed. What can I say? I'm providing a service.

"Four dollars seventy-five cents," I respond reluctantly, fully aware of what's coming next.

"Four seventy-five!?!" they say, sounding outraged and surprised all at once.

As I hustle down the steps, I stew over all of the annoying things that customers do:

- When I'm clearly selling dogs or pretzels, there's always some clown who asks, "Do you have beer?"
- There's always someone yelling out my item when my back is turned. After I come to a halt and do an about-face, the jokester pretends to watch the game.
- Someone always asks me the price. It's on my badge in plain sight. If you have to ask, it's too much. It *is* too much, but that's besides the point.
- Someone always doesn't have their money ready, and I have to waste valuable time waiting for them to scrounge through their belongings. When it's in their shoe, I'm in big trouble!
- Someone's always getting in my way. Please, treat me like a lady and grant me the right of way. I'm carrying a forty-pound aluminum case of dogs up a steep flight of stairs.
- Someone always thinks that I have the wingspan of an NBA player. After I sell you an item, hold your hand out, so I can hand you the item with relative ease.
- Someone always tries to unload their piggy bank on me. Small change is a bummer.
- Someone always feels as if I'm public property. Don't touch me. Wait patiently, say "excuse me," and I'll move.
- Someone always asks for ingredients. Who really knows what's in the pretzels—or the dogs, for that matter. Here are the ingredients, in short: IT'S CRAP!

After three hours, I'm drenched in perspiration and Iron Man's ice cubes, which have slid off the tray and onto me. I have sold one hundred waters on the button. I'm only making 13-plus percent commission. As far as a paycheck, it's not a particularly good day ($62). Of course, the dough is not my primary motivation. I wanted to experience spring training. Technically, this is my vacation. Perhaps I should go back to school—to learn how to vacation properly.

Following the game, in the restroom, I wait in the long line. Iron Man is next to me in an adjacent line. My line moves faster, so I tell Iron Man to go ahead and stream away. He smiles gratefully and does. We'd make wonderful candidates for a Flomax commercial.

The very next afternoon, I return for a game against the Phillies. Fortunately, my voice returns, too. Even in spring training, Phillies fans travel well, and the place is packed early. I request dogs, which weren't on the vendor menu the previous day. Dogs don't have a designated hawker yet, so they're granted to the tourist vendor. At City of Palms dogs prove to be a particularly good deal for vendors because they go for $4.25, and customers hand you a $5 and often tell you to keep the change. In vendor parlance, that's *great* subway. I'm funding this vacation! Also, they're pre prepared, already wrapped in aluminum foil, so there's no methodical assemblage. All in all, it's a cakewalk. I won't be killing myself as I did the previous day.

The dogs sell briskly, perhaps too briskly. In fact, Iron Man and his cohorts can't make them fast enough, and I'm stuck waiting around in the Pit. Soon enough, I learn the reason for my brisk sales: a flood has shut down the stadium's main concession stand. Now, people are begging to be fed, but they have nowhere to go—except to the sole dog vendor in the house. Obviously, these kind of malfunctions are a godsend for a vendor.

Meanwhile, Iron Man is struggling to prepare the dogs, so I'm recruited into dog preparation duty. I don tight plastic gloves and Iron Man orders me to place the dogs into tight, tubular aluminum foil bags, which aren't easy to open, especially with skin-tight gloves. Iron Man tells me to prop open the bag, as he attempts to demonstrate. But the bag refuses to open for him, and he stares at it dejectedly. Frustrated, Iron Man banishes me from dog preparation, to wait off to the side, which I gladly do. This is Iron Man's domain.

Eventually, the bags cooperate, and I hit the corridor with more rations, but don't get far. Immediately, I'm surrounded by desperate, famished customers. A few minutes later, I reload and am selling again. I sell dogs until there are none left. It's all right. It's around the eighth. I watch the last inning from a front row seat in left field. I can't remember the last time I sat to watch the end of a game. And when it comes to that, I'm no natural. It feels strange. In the stands, I have the need to serve. I force myself to ignore my vending instincts and just sit there for a few outs.

After an unwanted day off, I request dogs again and head out even earlier than the previous day, 11:30 a.m., an hour and a half before the first pitch. It's my last game, so I want to soak up as much of spring training as possible. It's a split squad game, which means half of the team is playing elsewhere. Also, the Sox are playing the Marlins, who don't travel particularly well. Soon enough, I learn this: many Sox fans start their drinking early, at least in spring training. My dog sales are decent but without the assistance of a flood, they aren't nearly as strong as the previous day. Also, the Sox are getting blown out, and it's starting to drizzle. It is a universal fact: rain and the home team getting trounced are ingredients for dreadful hawker sales. By the seventh, I can't sell a single dog, and I return my remaining dogs to the Pit. I hand in my vendor shirt, grab my bag, and exit City of Palms. I've got a plane to catch in a few hours. Such is the life of a tourist vendor.

13

Old-Fashioned Hardball

Like Brett Favre, I'm back again!

It's a Sunday night game at Citi Field. I usually avoid Sunday night games at all costs. They're made for television and turnout is usually light. This is no ordinary Sunday evening, though. Instead of the typical pop songs, an organ plays solemnly over the loudspeakers and fans hold plastic candles. It's the tenth anniversary of 9/11 and the mood is somber. Ten years earlier, in the first baseball game played in New York following the horrific tragedy, Mike Piazza hit a game-winning home run to bring a small piece of positivity to a heartbroken city.

During the few games I've worked this season, Citi has been a relative ghost town. The Mets are banged up and aren't a very good baseball team. In addition, the Mets' owners are being sued for hundreds of millions by the victims of Bernie Madoff. Here's the CliffsNotes version: the victims' attorney claims that the owners knowingly profited from Madoff's Ponzi scheme. Ultimately, the owners might have to sell a part of the team, if not all, and the entire episode has cast a pall over the season.

Tonight—in a surprising twist—concessions take center stage. Ten years earlier, the night of Piazza's memorable homer, the Mets wore the hats of the agencies (NYPD and FDNY, to name two) that were first to respond at the World Trade Center. For the anniversary, the team was planning on repeating the tribute, until Major League Baseball forbade it. (MLB had forbidden the initial tribute as well, but the players to their credit ignored the directive, and MLB ultimately took no action.) For the anniversary, the players obey the order, wearing the hats of the agencies in warm-ups but not during the actual game. The hat ban might have something to do with the fact that MLB is hawking 9/11 commemorative hats on their website for thirty-six bucks. Sadly, this episode overshadows the solemn evening at least in my mind. It feels wrong to be pushing overpriced pretzels to grief-stricken civil servants. More than ever, it feels right to retire my vending smock.

Promptly following the 9/11 game, the Mets, who have overachieved thus far, go on a losing tear.

———

For the 9/11 game, I wasn't at 100 percent physically. My pinky hurt! Let me explain.

I was still hurting from playing hardball the previous day. While conducting research on vintage baseball, which is hardball played by nineteenth-century rules, I landed an invitation to play with the New York Gothams. Despite the fact that I hadn't stepped on any type of diamond in years, I accepted. Surprise, surprise.

Hardball vintage style is truly hard ball. Vintage ballers play without gloves. I repeat: they play without gloves. In the very first inning of my debut, I discover I desperately need one. I'm playing second, and someone is attempting to steal. I run over to cover the bag, and the catcher whips the ball to me. Promptly, I become paralyzed. It's one thing when the hardball is soft-tossed somewhat delicately, like an egg. It's entirely another when someone is chucking it at you with everything they got, especially if you're a muffin, which is the unfortunate nickname vintage players assign to rookies such as myself. As the ball comes toward me, I see the runner charging toward the bag—and me.

And I panic.

I flinch.

I freeze.

At the crucial moment of convergence, I snake my arm around the runner, managing to get one measly finger on the ball. Of course I don't catch it. Unfortunately, my pinky hurts like hell. It's broken, though no one offers that diagnosis at the time. In not so many words, the message from my fellow Gothams: *It's swollen. Walk it off.*

So, for my debut double header, I score one broken pinky and no hits.

During my lowest of lowlights at the plate, I am desperately trying to keep a rally going. At the plate, I usually have a succinct conversation with myself that goes something like this: watch the ball come off the pitcher's fingertips, wait, and swing. Just as I am preparing to swing away, a Gotham breaks my concentration. "C'mon, muffin!" he yells repeatedly. Distracted, I overswing and wind up hitting a hard chopper up the middle, which somehow bounces off the pitcher's fingertips and on to his head. I run hard up the line. In vintage ball, they play ninety-foot base paths—none of this sixty-foot beer league, softball fluff. I beat the throw, but overrun the bag. Unfortunately, overrunning first is forbidden in vintage ball. After I run past first, the Gothams yell at me to return to the bag, and I do, diving headfirst into the bag, barely beating the first baseman's foot. I'm ecstatic! I got my first hit in vintage ball! Perhaps they won't call me a muffin anymore! My euphoria is short-lived. The umpire—dressed in nineteenth-century garb—calls me out for my base-running blunder. Sadly, he refuses to cut a muffin a break.

Three weeks later, I'm back at it with the Gothams—damaged pinky and all. We're in Delaware City, Delaware, competing in the vintage ball playoffs. Earlier in the week, I told the Gothams' captain that I wasn't worthy of a playoff roster spot. Basically, he told me to shut up and play. I'm grateful that he pushed me, but now I'm anxious. Catching line drives with no glove is unnerving—and then there's the Muffin moniker . . . As far as that, I'm partly to blame. When they asked me for my nickname, I offered up "Plimpton," which the Gothams didn't go for. Unfortunately, I'm stuck with Muffin. More bothersome than my Muffin moniker is my .000 batting average. I really want to get a hit, so in the days leading up to the game, I practice hitting a Wiffle ball.

In Delaware, we're playing on a retired navy base's quad. In our first-round game, a team from Maryland is playing us tough. When I get to the plate, we need a hit to keep a rally alive. Instead of giving myself my usual pep talk, I shut up and just hit.

And I do.

I bang a hard liner to right field. No doubt, it's gonna drop. But is it gonna drop enough? In vintage ball, catching a ball on one bounce is an out. As I hustle hard up the line, I watch the ball. It bounces once, and then the right fielder dives for it. He has it.

And then he doesn't. It bounces again. I got a hit! I got a hit!

I arrive at first base. I'm euphoric but don't let my emotions get the best of me. I stop immediately. I didn't get a home run. However, more important, I lost the Muffin moniker.

———

We wind up blowing a lead and the game. Then, we get blown out in the second game, which eliminates us from the playoffs. With the season over, it doesn't take long for this former muffin to become restless. I put my energies into seeing my manuscript published. It's easier said than done.

I get ignored.

I get rejected.

I get insulted. Repeatedly.

I pout.

I complain.

I quit.

But I always come back.

During this mapless journey, I was often as rudderless as a knuckle ball. But I've learned that you can never underestimate persistence. Not everyone has talent. But anyone can persist.

Finally, after months and months of pursuit—when I often felt like I was chasing Lance Armstrong on a tricycle—I got the e-mail that I had been vying for: an offer to publish my manuscript. It's a heck of a feeling.

OVERTIME

My blades are in the closet. Now, I bike. I don't attend professional sports events. However, when I watch on television, my eyes always gravitate to the hardworking, florescent bumblebees in the stands. (During tennis matches, I invariably study the technique of the ball persons.)

For the moment at least, I'm on the sidelines. I don't know if that's because I've been too consumed with writing or what.

Whatever happens, I do know that I will stare down my nemesis, the blank page, again. And it'll stare right back at me. We're two boxers in the center of the ring ready to throw down. When the bell rings, I'll type away. . . . Then again, I hear men's roller derby is making a big comeback.

ABOUT THE AUTHOR

Jon Hart has written for the *New York Times*, the *Christian Science Monitor*, and an array of outlets that have bit the dust. He graduated first in his class from mascot school. Then again, he was the only person in his graduating class. As a U.S. Open ball person, he was runner-up for Rookie of the Year. He has never been to the Olympics in any capacity, but he has done the Macarena with an Olympic gold medalist. He lives in New York City. Don't hold it against him.